Great
R·E·S·O·R·T·S
FOR PARENTS AND KIDS

**A Travel Guide to U.S. Resorts
with
Supervised Children's Programs**

Great R·E·S·O·R·T·S

FOR PARENTS AND KIDS

Written By

GAYLE BARKER
&
JOANNA PINICK

AN *EDITOR'S INK* TRAVEL GUIDE

Graphic Design: Rosemary Nulty

Maps: Boone Barker

Cover Photo: Courtesy of Club Med. All rights reserved.

Editor's Ink, 2802 E. Madison, Suite 117
Seattle, Washington 98112

Printed in the United States of America
First Editor's Ink Printing: September 1990
ISBN 0-9626380-0-5

To Amy with Love

Acknowledgements

Putting together a book like this takes more than a good idea and a lot of research. It takes the advice and perspective of many people. From the beginning we besieged our family and friends with our plans, ideas, and enthusiasm. We haunted book stores comparing travel guides and deciding what we liked and what we didn't. We surveyed friends and strangers alike about cover design, readability, format, and what they wanted from a travel guide in general, and a traveling with kids guide in particular. We thank them all for their excellent suggestions and support.

Thanks also to successful writers Bob Serling and Do Jasinek, to publisher Mal Stamper, and to travel agent Helene Spaulding of Greenlake Travel.

A special thank you, too, to the Resort and Commercial Recreation Association for helping us locate resorts with wonderful children's programs.

The most important thank you of all goes to our husbands, Boone Barker and Dan Pinick, for their support and good humor in the face of our preoccupation with "the book." We appreciate their patience, but most of all we thank them for their belief in our ability to do this without their comments, suggestions, or kibitzing except when we asked for it. Then their suggestions were practical, constructive, and knowledgeable. Didn't somebody say "a jewel beyond price is a supportive husband"? Well, something like that...

Contents

Introduction

What makes a Great Resort *Great*?

As an adult you might say *Great* is a challenging game of golf on a world class course, a thrilling tennis match, a few hours of horseback riding, romantic dinner cruises, or just relaxing by the pool with a good book. As a parent, sports and games with the kids, a western barbecue, fishing, or a special family adventure may be on the top of your list. If you ask your kids, they are probably looking for ACTION, a swim in the ocean, having their own horse for a week, playing with new kids, and having pizza for dinner.

The resorts in this book let you have it all!

We interviewed hundreds of resort managers and recreation staff members in order to find the rare combination of quality adult, child, and family activities. Although there are many wonderful resorts offering quality leisure time activities for adults, the seventy-four resorts listed in this guide also offer supervised children's programs of the caliber we were searching for. Specifically, we looked for programs that feel like a summer camp, are creative and varied, age-appropriate, and well supervised.

There is a wide range of resorts for you to choose from. Some offer seclusion; others, hustle and bustle. There are resorts in the desert, in the mountains, and on the beaches. A broad geographic mix from Kauai to Key West will let you choose just the right vacation for you and your family. A few are fancy coat-and-tie-for-dinner resorts, but most offer a choice from casual to elegant. Some of the resorts listed are year around resorts offering skiing during the winter months. But, if you are looking for a ski resort specifically, we suggest you contact you favorite ski area. Most offer junior ski programs as well as day care for younger children and infants.

The information for each resort has been reviewed and approved by the resort managers to make it as current and accurate as possible. A travel agent can help you with reservations and give you current rates, but we suggest you contact the resort directly with questions about their children's program. The programs can and often do change from season to season. If group size is important to you or your child, it is also a good idea to ask what is typical.

How This Book Is Organized

This book is divided into seven regions covering the continental U.S. and Hawaii. Each resort is listed geographically with a two page description in a consistent format, detailing the facilities, accommodations, supervised programs, and area attractions. You will find area maps in the index, as well as locations listed alphabetically by resort.

About Rates

Rates at vacation destinations vary widely depending upon the season and type of accommodations you choose. Packages almost always provide a more economical way to vacation if you are planning to use all the amenities that are included. Otherwise a straight nightly rate may be more economical. The rates in this book are intended to give you a feel for the relative price differences between the resorts we have included. We used summer rates, a family of four, and an average room as our standard. The dollar signs do not suggest a specific dollar amount. It is always best to check with a travel agent or write directly to the resort for the most current information.

Tips for Traveling with Kids

Normally when traveling with kids, getting there is not half the fun...but it can be more fun than you think with a little advance planning. Here are some suggestions and tips that we hope will make your trip more enjoyable.

Making your travel reservations: For the best fares, you will need to book well in advance. However, on a discounted ticket, seat assignments may be requested but are not guaranteed. Because many discount tickets now carry substantial penalties for cancelling or changing flights, it is also a good idea to review the refund policy before purchasing your tickets (particularly if having a sick child would cause you to want to change). Consider carefully the day of the week and time of day you wish to travel. Flight attendants are able to be more helpful and receptive to families during non peak times. So try to travel mid-week and mid-day if possible. You may request child and infant meals in advance, but it is best not to count on them.

Choosing your seats: Some things to consider are that bulkhead seats have no under seat storage, so you have to wait until the seatbelt sign is off before retrieving your carry-on items from the overhead compartment. If there is a movie, you will find yourself just inches from the screen. In general, children prefer to sit in the front row of a section for better movie viewing on the larger aircraft, or next to the window of smaller ones. To see outside, seats need to be away from the wing sections. Sound like a lot? It can be confusing, but most airlines will help you make a good choice for the aircraft they are using if you explain your situation. Once on the plane, it is a good idea to pay close attention to the emergency instructions. The flight attendants always tell you what to do for children.

Safety Seats: The Federal Aviation Administration (FAA) recommends using approved safety seats for infants on airplanes. The airline may charge you for a ticket for the additional passenger seat used, however. Because some airlines do not permit the use of any child safety seat, it is advisable to check with the airline you intend to use. Having the safety seat along will also give you the assurance that you will have one for your rental car on the other end. Most car rental agencies will not guarantee them.

Planning Your Flight: Perhaps the most important thing you can do is carefully plan what to carry on board. Basics are plenty of juice cartons, snack foods, diversions, a change of clothes for young children, cleanup supplies, and a favorite blanket for napping. If you freeze the juice before leaving, it will be cold when needed. If a child drinks during take-off and landing, it will help to clear their ears and shorten the wait time for snacks or meals. Finger snacks are a must, particularly if you need to fly during peak hours when the wait for food service can be quite long. It is also a good idea to pack valuable items, including prescription medicines, in your carry-on luggage.

Infants: If your family includes an infant, bassinets need to be requested when booking, and it is a good idea to bring a blanket along. Umbrella strollers can also be very useful when flying. They can carry not only children, but also carry-on bags down the long terminals, and fit easily into the overhead bins. Snugli also makes a Travel-All diaper bag that converts into a bed which fits on the floor between seats. A word of caution: infants do need to suck a bottle during take-off and landing to clear their ears.

Arrival at the Airport: If it is available, and it usually is, curbside baggage check-in is well worth the $1.00 per bag that it costs. You can proceed directly to the gate without waiting

4

in lines at the ticket counter. If you have a long connect time, an increasing number of airports across the country are offering designated play areas for children. Two that we know about are called "Kidport" and are located in Massport's Logan International Airport in Boston and Greater Pittsburgh's International Airport.

Boarding: Airlines almost always preboard families with small children. If the plane is not full, it may be better to wait until the last call before boarding. This will shorten the flight up to 20 minutes for the children. If the flight is full, you will need to board early to protect yourself from the possibility of duplicate boarding passes. Even if you have boarding passes, your seats can be resold to standbys if you have not checked in at least ten minutes before departure.

Diversions: Besides food and drink, children need lots of diversions. Packing a child's backpack with favorite "car" toys and games plus a few wrapped surprises and a couple of new coloring books can make the trip easier for everyone. A Walkman with story and music tapes is also a great diversion enjoyed by all children. On Delta flights, kids ages 2-12 can join the Fantastic Flyer™ Program at no cost and receive a Mickey Mouse visor and a copy of their Fantastic Flyer magazine filled with entertaining games, puzzles, stories, and fun facts about flying.

We hope this book will guide you to your best vacation ever!

Happy Landings!

Gayle Barker and Joanna Pinick

Hawaii

KAHALA HILTON

Address: 5000 Kahala Avenue, Honolulu, Hawaii 96816

Telephone: (800) HILTONS, or (808) 734-2211

Location: The Kahala Hilton is located between Diamond Head and Koko Head, 20 minutes from the Honolulu Airport and 10 minutes from Waikiki. Rental cars and limousine service are available.

Lodging: The Kahala Hilton offers 369 luxurious rooms and suites, with refrigerators in each room.

Rates: $$$$

For Parents

Poised on the edge of secluded Maunalua Bay, the Kahala Hilton is located in a beautiful residential area of Oahu that offers both seclusion and close proximity to the shopping and exciting entertainment of Honolulu. An exquisite white sandy beach dominates the shoreline in front of the hotel. An oceanfloat? A pedalboat? This resort is a wonderful place for you to relax, but if you prefer more active sports the resort will arrange all you need for snorkeling, windsurfing, catamaraning, and even kayaking. Several challenging golf courses are in the area for your enjoyment. The hotel's own spa is the Maunalua Bay Club, a two-acre, ocean-front tennis and fitness center located seven minutes from the Kahala Hilton via shuttle bus. The club is complete with six night-lighted tennis courts and staffed by nationally-ranked pros. The fitness center features saunas, Nautilus equipment, daily aerobic workouts, and a swimming pool. For excellent dining, four on-site restaurants offer a variety of cuisine and atmosphere. The Kahala Hilton is also the home of the long-running Danny Kaleikini Show (nightly except Sunday), one of Hawaii's best loved entertainers.

8

For Kids

Kamp Kahala, designed expressly for children, offers a fun filled activity oriented gathering for children of hotel guests. Experienced and caring junior hosts and hostesses are on hand each day. Activities include excursions to Sea Life Park, Honolulu Zoo, and the Honolulu Aquarium. There are also treasure hunts, picnics, hula lessons, movies, and lots of arts and crafts. A Junior Tennis Clinic is available at nearby Maunaulua Bay Tennis Club for a cost of $20, which includes a one-hour clinic for children six years and older, lunch, and shuttle transportation to and from the club.

Ages: 6-12 years old.

Days: Sunday through Saturday, Christmas and Easter holidays, and all of July and August.

Hours: 9:00 a.m. to 3:00 p.m. with a one hour lunch break (on own) from 11:30 a.m.to 12:30 p.m.

Cost: No charge for Kamp Kahala unless going on an excursion, then $17.00 which includes lunch, transportation and admission charge.

Area Attractions

Unique to the Kahala Hilton, the lagoon at the hotel has three Atlantic bottlenose dolphins that are fed three times daily. In addition, the Hilton has a couple of South African black-footed penguins in residence, as well as three large green sea turtles, a great collection of reef fish from local waters, two stingrays, and a moray eel.

Kapalua Bay Hotel

Address: One Bay Drive, Kapalua, Maui, Hawaii 96761

Telephone: (800) 367-8000, or (808) 669-5656

Location: The Kapalua Bay Hotel stands on Kapalua Beach in northwest Maui. It is most easily accessible from the West Maui airport, which is about 10 minutes away.

Lodging: Hotel rooms, suites, and villas are available. Villas are fully furnished private condominiums.

Rates: $$$$ Several packages are available.

For Parents

The Kapalua Bay Hotel and Villas are set in a secluded area on the northwest side of Maui. Beautiful beaches, great snorkeling, championship golf courses, and wonderful tennis are all on the grounds. Kapalua's golf holes wind through a wide variety of nature's backdrops. The Bay course features dramatic seaside fairways. Rising into the West Maui mountains, the Village Course travels through eucalyptus and ironwood trees, past a lake, and along high ridges. A third course, The Plantation, is scheduled to open in late 1990. For tennis lovers, a ten-court tropical garden tennis complex has a wealth of weekly activities for all levels. Tennis camps are offered from June to December. Its easy to see why this facility has been selected by Tennis Magazine as one of the 50 greatest U.S. tennis resorts. Water enthusiasts will enjoy the beautiful warm waters that surround Maui. The concierge can easily arrange snorkeling trips, windsurfing, sailing, and scuba diving excursions. Several great restaurants are on the premises, and shopping is nearby for those who prefer to dine in their villas. A diversity of evening entertainment is offered at the resort and in nearby Lahaina.

For Kids

The weekly Kamp Kapalua may include swimming and snorkeling, sand castle building, outdoor games, tennis clinics, nature hikes, arts and crafts, water sports, kite flying, field trips (tennis shoes required), a glassbottom boat cruise, and fishing. Children may choose desired activities from the weekly calendar of events, and specific plans are made each day with a counselor. The Kapalua Bay Hotel likes to keep the groups small (ratio: one counselor to five children), so reservations are required.

Ages: 6-12 years old.

Days: Monday through Friday throughout the summer, and Christmas and Spring school holidays.

Hours: 9:00 a.m. to 3:00 p.m., and 5:00 p.m. to 9:00 p.m.

Cost: $35 per child per day for the day session; $25 per child for the evening session.

Area Attractions

The historic whaling port of Lahaina and the Whaler's Village Museum is about 15 minutes away. The museum has a wonderful collection of artifacts to help us understand the history of whaling. Riding stables at Rainbow Ranch are nearby, as well as several excellent beaches favored by local people.

KONA VILLAGE

Address: P.O. Box 1299, Kailua-Kona, Hawaii 96745

Telephone: (800) 367-5290, or (808) 325-5555

Location: Kona Village is located on the Kohala Coast of the Island of Hawaii. It is 5.5 miles north of Keahole (Kona) Airport.

Lodging: There are 125 plush/primitive thatched bungalows in eight architectural styles representing the major island cultures of ancient Polynesia. No room phones, no television.

Rates: $$$$$ Full American Plan, all meals and activities included.

For Parents

Nestled between fingers of centuries old lava at the foot of Mount Hualalai, the Kona Village Resort resembles a village like those of the old South Pacific. Spaced for privacy, thatched bungalows perch on stilts by the ocean, a quiet beach, a lagoon, or in a lush garden setting. Natural sandy beaches and thousands of acres surround the resort to isolate it from the rest of the world. Here, you can do as much or as little as you like. Two fresh water swimming pools, Sunfish sailboats, outrigger canoes, snorkeling gear, glass-bottom boat excursions, boogie boards, float mats, three lighted tennis courts, volleyball, shuffleboard, and ping-pong are all included in the daily rate. Optional activities are available for a slight fee, such as catamaran sails, scuba diving, tennis lessons, deep sea fishing, and massages. Dining is at the Hale Moana, as well as in the intimate setting of the Hale Samoa. There are also weekly feasts featuring a paniolo steak fry and a lavish luau including kalua pig and poi. Nightly entertainment ranges from classical guitar to contemporary dance music.

For Kids

Children age six to 12 will find a wide choice of recreational activities and organized programs. A day's activities may include fishing contests, hula lessons, and finger painting. Children also learn about local marine life, how to play the ukulele, hunt seashells, fly kites, go stargazing, and participate in tennis tournaments. Teens are involved in snorkeling tours, volleyball games, canoeing, coconut tree climbing, tennis, or petroglyph field exploration. There are also special "children only" dinner seatings.

Ages: 6-12 years old, and teens; 5 and under when accompanied by an adult.

Days: Every day of the week, all year around.

Hours: 9:30 a.m. to 8:00 p.m.

Cost: Complimentary.

Area Attractions

The famous Parker Ranch is a short drive north, where you will find the Parker Ranch museum and shopping center. Sunset dinner cruises, glass-bottom boat tours, and whale watching expeditions (in season) depart daily from the wharf in Kailua; nearby are six 18-hole championship golf courses, horseback riding, and flightseeing tours.

MAUNA KEA BEACH HOTEL

Address: One Mauna Kea Beach Drive, Kohala Coast, Hawaii 96743

Telephone: (800) 882-6060, or (808) 882-7222

Location: The Mauna Kea is a 30 minute drive from Keahole Airport. Limousine service is available from the airport with advance request.

Lodging: The Mauna Kea has hotel rooms and suites. There is a three person per room maximum.

Rates: $$$$ Both Modified American Plan (two meals), and European Plan (no meals) are available.

For Parents

The Mauna Kea Beach Hotel, located on the Big Island, is surrounded by black lava outcropings, lush tropical vegetation, and white sand beaches. The championship golf course adjacent to the hotel is a Robert Trent Jones, Sr. design built on a 5,000 year old lava flow.   The holes provide both challenge and beauty. Some follow the curves of the shore, while others thread through the palms and around lava formations. Tennis is available on 13 oceanside courts separated by landscaping to provide privacy. Private or group lessons can be arranged, and the pro will assist with matches. When it's time for water play, the resort offers plenty. You can swim and sun in the freshwater pool overlooking the white sand beach or indulge in the many ocean activities available at your front door.   Windsurfers are available at the resort.   Deep sea fishing, snorkeling, and scuba diving trips can be easily arranged. The Big Island, because of its black lava, provides some of the most spectacular snorkeling and diving in the islands. There are five restaurants at Mauna Kea, providing great variety in cuisine and atmosphere, or you may choose to be served on your private lanai.

For Kids

The children's program at The Mauna Kea is supervised by experienced youth counselors who welcome children at the John Young Terrace for program registration each day at 8:30 a.m. Parents are required to accompany their children on the first day for registration. A typical summer program day might include sand sculpting on the beach, swimming at the beach or in the pool, a picnic, or a movie. Another day could have arts and crafts activities, games, shoreline exploration, or pole fishing. A treasure hunt, mini-Olympics on the beach, storytelling of Hawaiian legends, or coconut basket weaving might also be on the agenda.

Ages: 6-12 years old.

Days: Seven days a week for eleven weeks during summer months, three weeks during Christmas, and two weeks during Spring Break.

Hours: 8:30 a.m. to 4:30 p.m. (includes lunch), and 6:15 p.m. to 9:00 p.m.

Cost: Complimentary.

Area Attractions

The famous 250,000 acre privately-owned Parker Ranch is a short drive north. It has a museum, restaurants, and shops. You may wish to spend an entire day and drive south to Volcanoes National Park to view the latest lava outpourings from still-active Kilauea. Don't feel like driving? Tour companies schedule trips to The Big Island's main attractions. Sunset dinner cruises depart daily from the wharf at Kailua, as do glass-bottom boat tours, snorkeling expeditions, and whale-watching trips (in season).

MAUNA LANI BAY HOTEL & BUNGALOWS

Address: One Mauna Lani Drive, Kohala Coast, Hawaii 96743

Telephone: (800) 367-2323

Location: Fly into Keahole (Kona) Airport from Honolulu. You may arrange to be picked up, or car rental is available at the airport.

Lodging: Hotel rooms and suites are available, as well as a few ultra-deluxe two-bedroom bungalows.

Rates: $$$

For Parents

Mauna Lani Bay is in a truly spectacular setting. Sited on 3,200 acres of prehistoric black lava formations and tropical vegetation, the resort's natural beauty provides a wonderful setting for your dream Hawaiian vacation. The resort itself is a contemporary structure with its profile pointing directly out to sea. Most rooms focus on the beautiful blue Pacific Ocean. Golf at Mauna Lani is billed as one of the world's most remarkable golf experiences. Just yards from the Pacific, this course is built in and around the fascinating lava formations of the Kohala Coast. Hole number six actually crosses 180 yards of surging, open ocean. Tennis at the resort is on ten championship courts of varying speeds, and private lessons can be arranged to suit your schedule, or sign up for a clinic. Enjoying the warm waters of Hawaii is one of the greatest pleasures of the islands. You can indulge in a full complement of beach activities. Try diving, fishing, sailing, windsurfing, boat cruises, or just relaxing in the sun. Horseback riding and deep-sea fishing are nearby. Of course there are swimming pools, and you will also find a health club and jogging trails. Five restaurants on the premises provide a variety of cuisine, and one has live music for dancing until 11:00 p.m. nightly.

For Kids

Camp Mauni Lani Bay has a flexible program of games, sports, arts and crafts, swimming, and many other activities, all supervised by qualified counselors. A wide range of programs are planned that may include a scavenger hunt, pole fishing, historic tours, nature walks, photographic outings, outdoor games with prizes, or making Hawaiian gifts. Evening programs include movies, video games, or storytelling. Children may choose alternate activities on any given day. Those under five may also attend Camp Mauna Lani Bay if accompanied by a parent or sitter.

Ages: 5-12 years old.

Days: Daily throughout the summer, and during Christmas and Spring school holidays.

Hours: 9:00 a.m. to 3:00 p.m., and 5:30 p.m. to 10:30 p.m.

Cost: Complimentary (with the exception of video games, photography outings, lunch and dinner charges).

Area Attractions

The famous 250,000 acre privately-owned Parker Ranch is a short drive away, where you will find the Parker Ranch museum and shopping center. For the more adventuresome, there are helicopter tours of the ranch or a charter flight picnic into secluded Waipio Valley, where half a dozen waterfalls plunge over the valley's walls into verdant greenery below. Sunset dinner cruises depart the wharf at Kailua daily, as well as glass-bottom boat tours, snorkeling expeditions, whale-watching trips (in season), and submarine rides.

TURTLE BAY HILTON & COUNTRY CLUB

Address: P.O. Box 187, Kahuku, Oahu, Hawaii 96731

Telephone: (800) 445-8667, or (808) 293-8811

Location: This resort is on Oahu's North Shore. The shortest route is by way of Waimanalo. You may also go northward up the Windward Coast, along the North Shore, and across the Central Plateau for a more scenic route.

Lodging: The Turtle Bay Hilton offers both hotel rooms and privately-owned condominiums.

Rates: $$

For Parents

The Turtle Bay Hilton is unique because it is the only major resort on the north shore of Oahu. Although on the main island, it is far from the hustle and bustle, the noise, and the crowds of Honolulu. It is in a quiet area near excellent surfing beaches which can be seen from the windows of the hotel. On a five mile stretch of beach, the resort rambles into hidden coves, past the ironwood forest, and through undulating sand dunes. It is terrific for walkers. Many water activities, including catamaran cruises, boogie boarding, snorkeling, windsurfing, and scuba diving are awaiting your pleasure, along with lessons and equipment for all activities. Horseback riding is arranged with one telephone call. You will enjoy golf on the beautiful 18-hole, par 72 golf course. A lighted tennis and paddle sport complex offers a daily round-robin tournament. Aquacycling, jogging paths, kayaking, a sailing school, shuffleboard, guided walks, and volleyball are fun for all ages. Local artists and artisans demonstrate a variety of Hawaiian crafts in the hotel lobby Sunday through Saturday. Every Friday evening there is Hawaiian music in the lobby from 5:30 p.m. to 7:30 p.m.

18

For Kids

Hawaii

Activities for children seven years or older are available all year around with one-day advance notice. Hula and ukulele lessons, Hawaiian crafts instruction, nature walks and shell collecting expeditions, or shell art may be part of the morning session, while afternoons feature children's sports, like swimming, beach activities, kite flying, and croquet. Even though the supervised activities are of relatively short duration, we included this resort for those of you who wish to visit the Northshore of Ohau.

Ages: 7 years and older.

Days: Monday through Saturday during school holidays, and throughout the year on special request.

Hours: 9:00 a.m. to 10:00 a.m., and 2:00 p.m. to 3:00 p.m.

Cost: Complimentary with advance notice required.

Area Attractions

The Northshore has big winter surf (for seasoned experts only!), including the famous Banzai Pipeline. The nearby Polynesian Cultural Center condenses the vast span of Polynesia into walking distances, creating villages of Samoa, Tonga, Hawaii, Tahiti, Fiji, the Marquesas, and Maori New Zealand. Tours of the center, on foot or in an outrigger canoe, go on all day and evening, and are included in the admission price. There is an evening show each day at the Center. Waimea Falls Park (admission fee) is open from 10:00 a.m. to 5:30 p.m. daily. Open air minibusses wind through the botanical garden and arboretum of Waimea Valley to the breathtaking 45-foot waterfall.

19

THE WESTIN KAUAI-KAUAI LAGOONS

Address: Kalapaki Beach, Lihue, Hawaii 96766

Telephone: (800) 228-3000, or (808) 245-5050

Location: The resort is located on Nawiliwili Bay, outside Lihue, Kauai, just a mile from the airport and a mile and one-half from Lihue.

Lodging: The hotel has 846 guest rooms, including 41 suites and 46 Royal Beach Club rooms located in five towers.

Rates: $$$

For Parents

The Westin Kauai is located on an 800 acre resort called Kauai Lagoons. The resort is on beautiful Kalapaki Beach fronting Nawiliwili Bay on Kauai, the most tropical of the Hawaiian Islands. The lagoons are located 90 feet above sea level on a 500 acre plateau immediately behind the hotel complex. The spectacular manmade waterway system is 40 acres in size and is unique to the islands. Touring these lagoons is by outrigger canoe, or mahogany launch. A great way to explore the grounds is by horseback. Guided riding for all levels of ability is available. For golfers, the resort offers 36 spectacular holes of challenging golf in a beautiful setting. Both courses are signature courses of Jack Nicklaus, who is also the Director of Golf. Kauai Lagoons Racquet Club has eight plexipave tennis courts and a pro for instruction. The beach, of course, offers plenty of opportunity for sunbathing, and a multitude of other water sports. To tone up or just relax, the European Spa offers a Jacuzzi, massages, facials, exercise facilities, herbal wraps, steam baths, and saunas. There are ten restaurants in the resort complex and a variety of Hawaiian entertainment is offered daily. Each day, guests can take a sunset cocktail cruise on a 35-passenger launch along the lagoons.

For Kids

Camp Kalapaki offers a variety of activities. Half-day, three-quarter day, or full day sessions are available. All include appropriate meals. Reservations must be made prior to 9:00 a.m. the day before. The camp counselors have extensive experience in child care and elementary education. A sample of activities offered include pool activities, beach Olympics, lei making, wildlife tours, fill-in scrapbook, a crazy face painting party, sand castle building, torch lighting ceremony, Hawaiian food tasting, crafts, kid videos, carriage rides, storytelling, and nature walks.

Ages: 6-12 years old.

Days: Daily during the summer months, Christmas, and Spring school holidays.

Hours: 9:00 a.m. to 3:00 p.m. (includes lunch), 3:00 p.m. to 9:00 p.m. (includes dinner), or a full day program, 9:00 a.m. to 9:00 p.m. (includes lunch and dinner).

Cost: 1/2 day - $20; 3/4 day - $30; Full day - $40.

Area Attractions

The Kauai Museum in Lihue houses changing exhibits of Hawaiian art and an elaborate display of island history from its volcanic genesis to the end of the 19th century.

THE WESTIN MAUI

Address: 2365 Kaanapali Parkway, Lahaina, Hawaii 96761

Telephone: (800) 228-3000, or (808) 667-2525

Location: The Westin Maui is in the Kaanapali area, three miles west of Lahaina. Choose the West Maui airport, which is four miles from the resort.

Lodging: The Westin Maui has 761 rooms in a variety of configurations from single guest rooms to spacious suites. If more than one room is required a 25% discount from the room rate will apply to each room occupied by children.

Rates: $$$

For Parents

The Westin Maui is located on Kaanapali beach in the heart of the Maui resort area. The swimming pool at the resort looks like an Hawaiian fantasy with waterfalls, a slide that winds through a tropical forest, and thatched huts. The beach in front of the hotel stretches for miles, and snorkeling is excellent, with rental equipment and lessons available. Pool lessons in scuba diving are available for beginners or those who feel the need for a refresher. You can rent a Hobie Cat and sail it yourself , or go along for an accompanied ride if you would prefer. Windsurfing equipment is available for rent. Royal Kaanapali Golf Course offers 36 holes of challenging golf; free shuttle service is available. There is a complete tennis facility with 11 courts (six lighted for night play) and a well-stocked pro shop. A co-ed health club has weight training equipment and an exercise room, and aerobic and "aquacise" workouts are conducted daily. The five swimming pools and a swim-up Jacuzzi provide other fitness options. In the night-life department, all three of the on-site restaurants have live music nightly.

For Kids

The Westin Maui has an extensive seasonal supervised children's program. The staff of Keiki (Hawaiian for children) Camp plans a daily schedule that may include visits to Lahaina's Omni Theater to view "The Hawaii Experience," hikes to Black Rock Point, rides on the Sugar Cane Train, or movie parties. Or a typical day may feature a nature walk, art projects using materials collected on the walk, a trip to the library, a sailing cruise along the coastline in a 50-foot catamaran, or learning about the Hawaiian culture and how to make flower leis and ti-leaf skirts, or professional hula dancers may be on hand to teach the hula. One day advance reservations are required.

Ages: 5-12 years old.

Days: Monday through Friday throughout the summer months, Christmas and Easter weeks, and Wednesday, Thursday, Friday, and Saturday of Thanksgiving week.

Hours: 8:45 a.m. to 12 noon, and 12:45 p.m. to 4:00 p.m.

Cost: Morning program, $15 per child; afternoon program, $20 per child (includes lunch).

Area Attractions

The Sugar Cane Train, one of the most unusual attractions in the islands, is an 1890's-style, open-sided train of the Lahaina Kaanapali & Pacific Railroad; it chugs along a 6-mile route, taking you back 100 years when narrow-gauge trains were common on Hawaii's major islands. The Whaler's Village Museum in Lahaina is an excellent way to learn about old Hawaii's whaling industry.

West

THE ALISAL GUEST RANCH & RESORT

Address: 1054 Alisal Road, Solvang, California 93463

Telephone: (805) 688-6411

Location: The Alisal is forty miles north of the Santa Barbara airport in the Santa Ynez Valley near Solvang. About two hours from Los Angeles, car rental is available.

Lodging: With guest facilities for 200 people, accommodations range from large studio rooms with twin beds to two room suites or private three bedroom two bath bungalows, all with fireplaces.

Rates: $$ Modified American Plan (includes breakfast and dinner). There is a two night minimum. Golf, tennis, and horseback riding packages are available.

For Parents

Some come to Alisal for the horses, some come for the golf, but everyone comes for the calm, relaxing atmosphere. There is never a wait for tee times at the par 72 course, as it is reserved for guests and a few private club members. There are daily horseback trail rides. Seven tennis courts make lessons and clinics easy to schedule, and there is always court time. The recreation room has both pool and ping-pong tables. Outdoors, croquet, volleyball, and shuffleboard tournaments start up all the time. The pool and spa center are skirted by a generous lounging deck and luncheon snack bar for lazy hours in the sun. The nearby 100-acre lake is stocked with bluegill, catfish, and largemouth bass. Fishing gear is available. Sailboats, rowboats and windsurfing boards are available down at the lake. Sailing or windsurfing instructors are there if you need help. After dinner, The Oak Room Lounge has live entertainment nightly for dancing.

26

For Kids

Special activities for children are planned and supervised by a teacher from a nearby school with help from a staff of enthusiastic college students. This staff directs creative arts and crafts projects and active games throughout the day. Youngsters may engage in finger painting, clay modeling, penny dives, hikes, races, scavenger hunts, sand painting, ball games, story hour, or talent nights. There is an unsupervised playground for toddlers. Most evenings there are special programs for children, and in summer there are two children's dinners each week where children six to 16 years old may take their meals separately with a counselor. Golf and tennis clinics and lessons can be arranged for older children and teens for a fee.

Ages: 5-12 years old (some younger children may be allowed to participate).

Days: Daily throughout the summer and at Christmas and Easter school holidays.

Hours: 10:00 a.m. to 4:00 p.m.

Cost: Complimentary.

Area Attractions

The community of Solvang, originally settled by a group of Danes in the early 1900's, is a mecca for shoppers, with a wide variety of shops. The Santa Ynez Valley is a wine producing area, with a dozen or more wineries nearby. There is repertory theater in Solvang all summer long at Theatrefest.

INN OF THE SEVENTH MOUNTAIN

Address: P. O. Box 1207, Bend, Oregon 97709

Telephone: (800) 452-6810 in the West, or (503) 382-8711

Location: The Inn of the Seventh Mountain is about a 30 minute drive from the Redmond/Bend airport. Car rental is available. Van service from the airport can also be arranged in advance.

Lodging: Bedroom units at the inn sleep one to four people, while Fireside Studios sleep two to four people and include a living room, kitchenette, fireplace, and deck. Condominiums have one, two, or three bedrooms.

Rates: $$ Packages are available that include Mt. Bachelor ski lift tickets in winter, or whitewater rafting in summer.

For Parents

In winter you'll have fun skiing, ice skating, or taking snow-mobile tours; enjoy a brisk horseback ride, a sleigh ride, or a heated pool. In summer, tennis clinics and mixer tournaments are scheduled on the seven plexi-pave courts, as well as unlimited free court time. You can learn pickleball (a blend of tennis and ping-pong), with courts and equipment available for your use. Full day guided whitewater raft trips on the Deschutes River, and two hour river float trips are planned daily in 12-foot canoes, a 12-foot family raft, or a paddle drifter. A 28-foot river touring boat offers lunch and dinner excursions. There is a volleyball court and a putting green, a miniature golf course, and miles of jogging trails. Besides all that, there are two swimming pools, three spas, and a coed sauna. For golfers, a number of good courses are a short drive away. Activities like fitness classes, art, sports and games are scheduled daily for the whole family.

For Kids

Camp 7 Day Camp is for children four to eleven years old. It is either full day or half day. Supervised activities follow a daily theme to include arts and crafts, games, relay races, swimming at the pool, story hikes, pee wee races, or any number of other creative diversions for youngsters. For teens, there is softball, basketball, soccer, volleyball, and other scheduled activities planned by the recreation director. Time, place, and cost are published weekly in "This Week at the Inn." In addition, there are great family activities scheduled each day, like a 5:00 p.m. horsedrawn hayride. Two modern playgrounds are designed for kids, with safety in mind.

Ages: 4-11 years old.

Days: Daily.

Hours: 9 a.m. to 12:30 p.m., and 9:00 a.m. to 4:30 p.m. An evening program is available from 6:00 p.m. to 9:30 p.m.

Cost: Half Day, $9 per child; Full Day, $20 per child (includes lunch).

Area Attractions

Nearby, the western theme town of Sisters features the Sisters Rodeo and many quaint shops. The High Desert Museum has a wonderful history of Oregon settlers, plus an outdoor refuge for otters, fish, birds, and snakes. The Deschutes National Forest offers the more adventuresome opportunities for hiking, fishing, boating, horseback riding, and some of the finest cross-country skiing in the area. Lava Lands gives a visitor a chance to see the remains of volcano eruptions in Central Oregon and a mile long cave.

MARRIOTT'S RANCHO LAS PALMAS

Address: 41000 Bob Hope Drive, Rancho Mirage, California 92270

Telephone: (800) I LUV SUN, or (619) 568-2727

Location: The resort is a 20 minute drive from the Palm Springs Airport. Rental cars and limousine service are available.

Lodging: There are 456 hacienda-style rooms with separate sitting areas and patios.

Rates: $$ Several packages are available.

For Parents

The beautiful snow-capped San Jacinto Mountains offer a striking contrast to the resort's tropical landscaping and beautiful palm trees. The architecture is early California Mission style, with Mexican and Spanish accents. There is plenty for you to do here without ever leaving the premises. Recreational facilities include 27 holes of golf, 25 tennis courts (including three red clay courts), two swimming pools with spas, and a complete fitness center with universal weight machines and Saturday aerobics classes. The three distinctive golf courses at Rancho Las Palmas are known as the West, North, and South courses, and may be played in any combination for 18 holes. Each course offers a challenging yet enjoyable game for golfers at all levels. Lessons are available year around, and there is an on-site weekly golf school Monday through Friday from 8:00 a.m. to 3:00 p.m. For an afternoon of upscale shopping, the El Paseo shopping promenade, known locally as the Rodeo Drive of the Desert, is nearby. There are a number of good dining choices at the resort ranging from casual to elegant. In the evening, there is live entertainment and dancing in the lounge each Tuesday through Sunday.

For Kids

Children's programs at Rancho Las Palmas are offered during the morning only by the staff of the resort activities department. Kactus Kids provides a variety of activities for children six to twelve years old, and may include crafts, sports and games, swimming, and duck feeding. During the summer months, lunch is included.

Ages: 6-12 years old.

Days: Daily during the summer months and major holidays, and weekends during the rest of the year.

Hours: 9:30 a.m. to 1:00 p.m. during the summer, and 9:30 a.m. to 12:00 noon during the winter.

Cost: Complimentary.

Area Attractions

For families, there is an indoor ice-skating rink at Palm Desert Town Center. There are also hot air balloon rides, horseback riding, and celebrity home tours in the area. Disneyland® is less than a two hour drive away, as are all the family attractions of Southern California like Sea World, Universal Studios, Knotts Berry Farm, and on and on.

NORTHSTAR-AT-TAHOE

Address: P.O. Box 2499, Truckee, California 95734

Telephone: (800) 533-6787, or (916) 562-1113

Location: Forty miles from Reno via Interstate 80, car rental is available at Reno's airport. Privately owned or charter aircraft may fly into the Truckee-Tahoe Airport, and with notice Northstar will provide shuttle transportation.

Lodging: Both hotel rooms and condominium accommodations are available, as well as private homes. Condominiums and homes have up to four bedrooms. All have fully-equipped kitchens.

Rates: $$ Several packages are available.

For Parents

In winter, Northstar is a ski resort, with both downhill and cross-country skiing packages that include rooms plus lift tickets, instruction, and equipment rental. In summer, other activities abound. Golf, flyfishing, tennis, horseback riding, and fitness programs are the major attractions. Northstar has its own 18-hole championship golf course, and there are ten excellent tennis courts. Golf schools, flyfishing schools, and tennis camps are offered all summer long. Or, you may prefer to just relax and unwind by the pool and soak up the sun. A hike through the pine forests is exhilarating, or shop in the historic logging town of Truckee. Of course nighttime in Tahoe brings the excitement of the casinos just across the border in Nevada with 24 hour gaming and entertainment. For dining, you may enjoy a quiet outdoor patio dinner in Northstar's Village Mall, or a sunset dinner cruise on beautiful Lake Tahoe. There is also a wide variety of excellent restaurants at Northstar and in the general area, many with entertainment into the wee hours.

For Kids

During the ski season, Minors' Camp is a fun place to spend the day. It is filled with activities like art, drama, science projects, singing, storytelling, kid's cooking, walks and field trips, or outdoor snow play. In addition, there is a learn-to-ski option for children three through six, which includes equipment, lunch, and two snacks, plus the hour and a half lesson. At other seasons of the year, Northstar's Minors' Camp has the same diversions, except instead of snow play there are games and fun in the sun in the pool.

Ages: 2*-10 years old during the summer and 2*-6 during the winter (*children must be toilet trained).

Days: During the summer, Monday through Saturday. Daily during the winter.

Hours: Winter program is 8:00 a.m. to 4:30 p.m., or 12:45 p.m. to 4:30 p.m.; summer program is 9:00 a.m. to 5:00 p.m.

Cost: The winter program is $30 per child for the full day, or $20 per child for the afternoon session, and the summer program is $3.00 per hour plus $2.00 for lunch for each child, and occasional fees for outings. For additional children in the same family, the charge is $2.00 per hour.

Area Attractions

Sunday outdoor brunch and jazz concerts are held in the Village Mall. Boating, board sailing, and water skiing on Lake Tahoe, Donner Lake, and Boca Reservoir are nearby. Fishermen will enjoy the variety of streams, rivers, and lakes offering rainbow, German brown, brook, and lake trout. River rafting on the Truckee River in summer is fun for everyone.

RANCHO BERNARDO INN

Address: 17550 Bernardo Oaks Drive, San Diego, California 92128

Telephone: (800) 854-1065, (800) 542-6096 in California, or (619) 487-1611

Location: Rancho Bernardo Inn is 28 minutes from the San Diego International Airport. There is van service to and from the airport with 24 hour notice. It is about a two and a half hour drive from Los Angeles.

Lodging: There are 287 rooms, including 58 one and two bedroom suites. All suites have refrigerators and wet bars.

Rates: $$ Special golf and tennis packages are offered.

For Parents

Rancho Bernardo Inn is a beautiful, luxurious tennis and golf resort with an early California ranch feeling. It reflects that era's spirit of warm hospitality in its artifacts, art collection, and 265 acres of rambling, landscaped grounds nestled in the San Pasqual Mountains. Besides the challenging par 72 championship golf course, you will find three 9-hole executive courses to ensure a variety of play and to accommodate every ability. There are 12 tennis courts, four lighted for nighttime play. A continuing Tennis College offers mixers, private lessons, and clinics. Their well stocked pro shop is court-side. The fitness center has a fully equipped workout room with state-of-the-art weights, treadmill, stairmaster, cycles, saunas, steam rooms, massage, and the advice of a personal weight trainer. There are two large swimming pools at Rancho Bernardo Inn with food and cocktail service available poolside, and seven whirlpool baths, a driving range, bicycling, ping-pong, and volleyball.

For Kids

Rancho Bernardo Inn has a well established program for children. It is run by child care professionals with an imaginative hands-on approach. Unfortunately this program is offered only five times a year. Some of the activities that are part of the daily Children's Camp include scavenger hunts, cookouts and campfires, miniature golf, kite making and flying, water games, croquet, and ice cream making. Other activities include swimming, arts and crafts, soccer, basketball, hockey, softball, and other sports. Saturday cartoon breakfasts, "kidercize," children's casino nights, storytelling, cards and table games, track meets, movies, carnivals, luaus, and field trips are also scheduled. Teens through the age of 17 have a program structured around their needs and interests as an older group.

Ages: 4-17 years old, divided into age groups.

Days: Ten days at Easter, ten days at Christmas, the 4th of July and Thanksgiving weekends, and the entire month of August.

Hours: 9:00 a.m. to 9:00 p.m.

Cost: Complimentary except for meal costs and occasional field trip expenses.

Area Attractions

Nearby attractions include Sea World, the San Diego Zoo, Wild Animal Park, Pacific Ocean beaches, Balboa Park, Del Mar Racetrack, Mt. Palomar Observatory, and Disneyland.

ROCK SPRINGS GUEST RANCH

Address: 64201 Tyler Road, Bend, Oregon 97701

Telephone: (503) 382-1957

Location: Rock Springs is nine miles northwest of Bend in central Oregon. It is a two to three hour drive from Portland, Salem, and Eugene. The Redmond Municipal Airport is about 13 miles northeast of the ranch, and is served by several airlines. Rental cars are available at the airport.

Lodging: Private cabins accommodate guests (limited to 50 reservations at a time). Most cabins have a fireplace, and each has a deck.

Rates: $$$ Full American Plan during the summer, or Modified American Plan (selected holidays).

For Parents

Of all the sports in the great outdoors, horseback riding is truly what they put their hearts into at Rock Springs. With 65 special guest horses, the perfect horse is waiting for you. Beginning riders enjoy the terrain at a pace that progresses daily. More experienced riders take the trails at a faster clip and explore the Ponderosas in their own group. Besides the horseback riding program, there is tennis, croquet, badminton, volleyball, horseshoes, ping-pong, pool, swimming, and a whirlpool spa. Off the ranch, golf, windsurfing, fly fishing, and whitewater rafting are all available nearby. Meals at the ranch are served in the main lodge or at outdoor barbecues. During the day guests help themselves to homemade cookies, fresh fruit, and beverages in the lodge dining room. At lunch and dinner children may choose their own dining area, and at 5:30 adults may gather on the deck for delicious hors d'oeuvres and a variety of northwest wines and imported and domestic beers.

For Kids

The activity program for children is run by well qualified counselors who are carefully screened upon application. They must have previous experience in youth counseling, and provide reliable references. People chosen are young at heart, love working with children, and are enthusiastic and imaginative. With this sort of guidance, children have fun learning about the outdoors and the west. Some of the activities planned for them may be a hayride, staging a talent show, or participating in a variety of arts, crafts, and sports. A carefully structured horseback riding program for kids is a main attraction, with instruction by a special kid's wrangler who will help them enjoy daily improvements in skill, proficiency, and confidence.

Ages: 5-12 years old.

Days: Daily during the summer.

Hours: 9:00 a.m. to 1:00 p.m., and 5:00 p.m. to 9:00 p.m.

Cost: Complimentary.

Area Attractions

Nearby, the western theme town of Sisters features the Sisters Rodeo, and many quaint shops. The Deschutes National Forest offers the more adventuresome opportunities for hiking, fishing, boating, horseback riding, and some of the finest cross-country skiing in the area in winter.

SUNRIVER LODGE

Address: P.O. Box 3609, Sunriver, Oregon 97707

Telephone: (800) 547-3922

Location: Sunriver Lodge is 15 miles south of Bend on Highway 97. There is air service to the Redmond/Bend airport, and car rental and limousine service are available. Sunriver Lodge is also accessible by private plane via the resort's 5,500 foot airstrip.

Lodging: Sunriver offers a variety of accommodations from bedrooms and suites to private resort homes and condominiums.

Rates: $$

For Parents

It is called Sunriver, and it certainly lives up to its name. Located on the sunsplashed side of Oregon's Cascade Mountains near the Deschutes river, Sunriver offers you and your family a wide range of activities throughout the year. During the summer there are two 18-hole championship golf courses, tennis, racquet ball, swimming, bike riding, whitewater rafting, canoeing, fishing, and horseback riding, plus miles of trails for jogging and strolling. When the snow falls, Sunriver transforms into a ski village with convenient shuttle service to neighboring Mt. Bachelor. On the grounds of Sunriver you will be able to ice skate, take a ride in a horsedrawn sleigh, try cross country skiing, jump in a hot tub, or indulge yourself with saunas and massages. For dining, sample elegant cuisine at The Meadows, stop by the The Provision Company for a meal or snack, or head for the Owl's Nest for live nightly entertainment. If you rent a condominium, there is shopping at the Sunriver Village Mall. The mall has over 50 shops and restaurants.

For Kids

The Kid's Klub at Sunriver is a carefully structured, broad based program of activities developed to enhance a child's personal and social growth while giving ample opportunity to enjoy all the excitement the resort has to offer. The coordinator is a state-certified teacher with wide experience in outdoor recreation programs. The staff is comprised of undergraduates in elementary education and recreation management. All members are trained in First Aid and CPR. Depending on the season, children choose from a variety of activities like horseback riding, swimming in the pool, and water games. Canoeing, pond dips, tennis, volleyball and badminton, field games, nature hikes, photography, arts and crafts, and feature movies are all part of the fun.

Ages: 5-12 years old.

Days: Monday through Saturday, mid-June to Labor Day, and the Christmas, New Year's, and Spring break school holidays.

Hours: Session I: 9:00 a.m.to 12:00 noon (plus a one-hour optional lunch). Session II: 1:00 p.m. to 4:00 p.m. Session III: 6:30 p.m. to 9:30 p.m.

Cost: $11.00 per child, per session, $5.00 for lunch or bring your own. Discounts to families with more than one child.

Area Attractions

Nearby, the western theme town of Sisters features the Sisters Rodeo, and many quaint shops. The Deschutes National Forest offers the more adventuresome opportunities for hiking, fishing, boating, horseback riding, and some of the finest cross-country skiing in the area.

SUN MOUNTAIN LODGE

Address: P.O. Box 1000, Winthrop, Washington 98862

Telephone: (800) 572-0493 or (509) 996-2211

Location: Sun Mountain Lodge is a four hour drive from the Seattle-Tacoma International Airport or about half of that from Wenatchee's Pangborne Field. Rental cars are available at both airports.

Lodging: All resort rooms offer spectacular views and are available in single, double, or triple bed configurations. Cabins are also available at Patterson Lake. They are equipped with a kitchenette, fireplace, queen bed and a hide-a-bed.

Rates: $$ Children 12 and under stay free in parent's room.

For Parents

Sun Mountain Lodge has a truly spectacular setting! Perched at the 3,000 foot level above the Methow River Valley in the North Cascade Mountains, there is breathtaking scenery everywhere. Snowcapped mountain peaks, clear mountain lakes, and lush green meadows abound. Wondering about rain? With the Cascades to the west serving as a natural barrier, the area receives an average of only 15 inches of rainfall a year, and most of that in the form of snow during the winter months. Recreation can be just about anything you would like it to be. Tennis courts, two hot tubs, a swimming pool, rafting, fishing, golf (at nearby Bear Creek Golf Course), and horseback riding are all available. There is also a mountain lake with boat and canoe rentals. During the winter months, over 50 miles of cross-country ski trails from easy to expert begin at the Lodge's door. Dining is in the Lodge or at the poolside cafe.

40

For Kids

Sun Mountaineers, lead by an enthusiastic and skilled staff, is a nature activity program for children ages 5-12 years old. Headquarters for the children's activities is in an authentic tee-pee. The program gravitates around nature walks, sports and games, and nature oriented arts and crafts. The counselors may provide the children with materials to build bird houses and then they can hang them at the beaver pond, possibly seeing a beaver or two! Most afternoons are spent at Patterson Lake, fishing, playing games, or just splashing in the water. The evening session includes an activity and dinner.

Ages: 5-12 years old.

Days: Daily from the end of June through Labor Day.

Hours: Session I: 9:00 a.m. to 12:30 p.m.(includes lunch and a T-shirt); Session II 1:00 p.m. to 3:30 p.m.; Session III: 6:00 p.m. to 9:00 p.m. (includes dinner).

Cost: Session I - $27.50; Session II - $12.00; Session III - $19.00.

Area Attractions

Historic Winthrop is only a short drive away. Once a bustling gold mining town, it has been returned to its colorful 1890's origin with barnwood storefronts, hitching posts, and clapboard sidewalks.

Rocky Mountain

Colorado Trails Ranch

Address: P. O. Box 848, Durango, Colorado 81302

Telephone: (303) 247-5055

Location: The ranch is a 20 minute drive from the Durango airport. Ranch staff will meet your plane and deliver you back to the airport at the end of your stay.

Lodging: There are Alpine, country, or mountain style cabins to choose from.

Rates: $$$$ Rates are weekly, Full American Plan, and include all meals, activities, and the use of the horses.

For Parents

The ranch's 525 acres and the adjacent San Juan National Forest will put you right in the middle of one of the prettiest parts of the Colorado Rockies. The ranch takes full advantage of its location. Each of the guest cabins is nestled in a private area providing beautiful views. There are miles and miles of trails for riding, of course, but there is also tennis, swimming, volleyball, softball, hiking, basketball, shooting sports, and just plain loafing. The archery, riflery, and trap shooting ranges are supervised, and instruction is available. Rifles, shotguns, and bows and arrows can be provided for your use. If you wish, you can bring your own. A weekly pool party on Saturday afternoons and a whirlpool spa for therapeutic relaxation are designated adults only. In the evenings, musical shows, square dancing, cookouts, and hayrides entertain the whole family. Because of Colorado State liquor laws, there is no bar at the ranch, and alcoholic beverages may be consumed in the cabins only.

Rocky Mountain

For Kids

Children and teens keep busy each day with the activities they most enjoy. Three fully-supervised groups for young guests, each with its own counselor and a flexible program designed to insure maximum fun and participation, are offered. Horseback riding lessons and games are a large part of the program. The riding staff is careful to choose the right horse for each child and provide the proper methods for giving commands to the horse. Swimming, water skiing, shooting sports, and tennis are some of the other activities offered. There is also a large "ruckus room" with games of all kinds for a between-activities gathering place for children of all ages.

Ages: 5-9 years old, 9-13 years old, and 13-18 years old.

Days: Monday through Saturday, early June through late August.

Hours: 8:15 a.m. to noon, 2:15 to 5:30 p.m., and 8:15 a.m. to 10:00 p.m.

Cost: Complimentary

Area Attractions

Ride the Durango and Silverton narrow gauge railroad through the Animas River canyon to Silverton, or visit Mesa Verde National Park which once housed a stone-age civilization of cliff dwelling Indians.

DROWSY WATER RANCH

Address: P.O. Box 147, Granby, Colorado 80446

Telephone: (303) 725-3456

Location: The ranch is 90 miles west of Denver near Granby, Colorado. Granby is served by Amtrac, and the ranch has pick-up and delivery service.

Lodging: Accommodations are in a main lodge and separate small log cabins.

Rates: $$$$ Rates are weekly, Full American Plan, and include all meals, activities, and the use of the horses.

For Parents

Drowsy Water is a genuinely rustic (but modernized), relaxed, comfortable ranch located amid the beautiful Rocky Mountains. The ranch buildings are sheltered in stands of aspen and pine overlooking Drowsy Water Creek. There is lots to do here. Horseback riding, trout fishing, golf (at nearby Grand Lake), hiking, and jeep trail rides are popular pastimes. Swimming, volleyball, horseback arena games, square dancing, songfests, pack trips, and river raft trips are all part of your week at Drowsy Water. You may partake of as many or as few of the activities as you wish. If just lazing around in the sun while the rest of the family enjoys the great outdoors is your idea of a perfect vacation, then Drowsy Water may be just the place for you. Most of the family-style meals are served in the main lodge, but there may also be cookouts and trail breakfasts from time to time. After dinner there is often a hayride with a songfest, or toasted marshmallows and hot chocolate around a blazing fire. One evening a week the talented staff of Drowsy Water stages some grand entertainment for the whole family.

For Kids

Children of five and under (except infants) are entertained by their own counselor with "riding" horses around the ranch, playing games, going on nature hikes, creating crafts projects, and other planned activities. Children from six to 13 are instructed in proper horsemanship and go on trail rides together. After riding, a counselor leads the way to games, archery, fishing, nature hikes, swimming, arts and crafts, or obstacle course races to name just a few of the planned activities. There is a children's hayride on one evening. On other evenings, there may be a carnival, movies or other fun activities.

Ages: 3-5 years old, and 6-13 years old.

Days: Sunday through Sunday during the summer months.

Hours: 9:15 a.m. to 8:00 p.m.

Cost: Complimentary.

Area Attractions

Boating and fishing are available at Grand Lake, Shadow Mountain Lake, and Granby Lake. The nearby Colorado River offers rainbow and brown trout. The ranch is also close to Rocky Mountain National Park for hiking and picnicking.

FLATHEAD LAKE LODGE

Address: P. O. Box 248, Bigfork, Montana 59911

Telephone: (406) 837-4391

Location: The ranch lies just outside Kalispell, Montana, and is served by several major airlines. Amtrack serves Whitefish, Montana, and transportation to the ranch can be arranged from either location. Rental cars are available in Kalispell.

Lodging: Guest capacity is about 100, housed in two and three bedroom cottages for families; lodge rooms accommodate singles and couples.

Rates: $$$$ Rates are weekly, Full American Plan, and include all meals, activities, and the use of the horses.

For Parents

Flathead Lake Lodge is in western Montana right on the shores of the largest natural lake west of the Great Lakes. The lodges, built in 1932, are log cabin style and are the center for activity and dining. Whether you are novice or expert, there is horseback riding on the remote, unspoiled mountain terrain, around the ranch, or horse games in the riding arena. Breakfast rides and cook-outs over an open fire and even rodeos are frequently on the agenda. As an added attraction, this dude ranch also has lake cruises, water-skiing, tennis, canoes, fly fishing, and sailing. There are three golf courses within 30 minutes of the ranch. You can swim in the lake or in the heated pool, try an innertube float on the nearby Swan River, or whitewater raft on the Lower Flathead. Evenings, enjoy a beach fire and singalong under the stars, or mosey into the village for live theater or dancing. Or simply relax and dream before the huge stone fireplace in the lodge with the last cup of coffee of the day.

48

For Kids

Days begin with a children's breakfast seating at 8:00 a.m., followed by horseback riding for those over six. Younger children are saddle-pals with the wranglers, and get to ride along. For older children, riding instruction is available, as well as the planned activities. These may include arts and crafts (with projects like pine-cone cowboy construction), games, or nature hikes. After lunch, water sports are usually organized, with swimming, windsurfing, boogie boarding, or water skiing on the lake. Optional afternoon activities for kids over seven are innertubing and whitewater rafting at nearby sites. Each Friday evening a children's overnight campout is planned. All activities are well supervised by several of the college students employed each summer by the ranch. One of the highlights of each week is a kid's rodeo, featuring barrel racing, egg races, sack races, and other fun events.

Ages: 3 years old and up.

Days: Monday through Saturday, June to mid-September.

Hours: 8:00 a. m. to 10:00 p.m.

Cost: Complimentary.

Area Attractions

Glacier National Park is just 35 miles away. National Bison Range is a one hour drive, Jewel Basin hiking area is a half hour. Big Mountain is just one hour away and runs a lift during the summer months. The views are spectacular!

LAKE MANCOS RANCH

Address: 42688 County Road N., Mancos, Colorado 81328

Telephone: (303) 533-7900

Location: Lake Mancos Ranch is 250 miles from Albuquerque, and 400 miles from Denver. Several commuter airlines serve the area, and the ranch will meet your plane in Durango or Cortez.

Lodging: There are 14 guest cabins with two or three bedrooms each, as well as accommodations for couples or singles in the guest wing of the ranch house.

Rates: $$$ Rates are weekly, Full American Plan, and include all meals, activities, and the use of the horses.

For Parents

Lake Mancos Ranch is in cattle country, about five miles above the little ranching town of Mancos. The ranch perches on a beautiful plateau (elevation 8,000 feet) adjacent to the San Juan National Forest, and has views of the La Plata Range, with rugged silver peaks over 13,000 feet high. There are two fishing areas right on the ranch where lively mountain trout make fishing an experience to remember. Fly fishing instruction is available if you want it, and you can schedule a trip to nearby McPhee Dam for some truly outrageous fishing! Riding instruction and trail rides, horseback exploration of the magnificent high country, swimming, and four-wheeling are all part of the fun. Abundant wildflowers in the area make photography and nature hikes unusually rewarding. A hot tub, ping-pong, horseshoes, and a library are available for your spare moments. Ranch meals are wonderful, and cookouts in Rendezvous Canyon are fun expeditions for the whole family.

For Kids

Supervised activities are provided during the mornings, evenings, and most afternoons. Daytime activities center around the horses. Four and five year olds are led around on gentle horses, or they go to the playground while older children are riding. Later, the groups join together for fishing, hayrides, hot dog cookouts, lawn games, firesides, movie parties, hikes or scavenger hunts. The children's program is flexible and geared to the specific interests of the group. For older children, the ranch offers a flexible program where they choose activities from a number of options. These special outings may include a mountain hike, a taco party, a jeep ride, volleyball, a ping-pong tournament, or even an overnight campout.

Ages: 4-12 years old divided into three age groups.

Days: June through August.

Hours: Varies depending on the activities for the day.

Cost: Complimentary.

Area Attractions

Ride the Durango and Silverton narrow gauge railroad through the Animas River canyon to Silverton. See Mesa Verde National Park which once housed a stone-age civilization of cliff dwelling Indians.

LONE MOUNTAIN RANCH

Address: P. O. Box 69, Big Sky, Montana 59716

Telephone: (406) 995-4644

Location: Bozeman is the closest airport to the ranch. Airport shuttle is provided, or car rental is available at the airport.

Lodging: A main dining lodge, and one and two room log cabins.

Rates: $$$ Rates are weekly, Full American Plan, and include all meals, activities, and the use of the horses.

For Parents

Lone Mountain Ranch was one of the first ranches in the Gallatin Canyon and it is steeped in the rich traditions of early ranch life. Snuggled against the Spanish Peaks in the heart of Yellowstone country, this ranch provides a scenic, uncrowded environment for your relaxation and enjoyment. When you think of the west and Montana, probably one of the first images that comes into your mind is one of cowboys and horses. Horses are a way of life on the ranch. There are guided trail rides for all skill levels twice a day except Sunday. Several all-day horseback trips will be planned, and at least once a week horses are trailered to a remote trailhead so you can explore the spectacular backcountry. Back at the ranch, the large Jacuzzi hot tub will help to get the kinks out after a day of riding. For those who prefer a little non-horse diversion, the ranch's naturalist program offers interpretive trips to Yellowstone, wildflower walks, orienteering, and birding. The Big Sky area near the ranch has golf, tennis, whitewater rafting, rock climbing, and swimming. Some evenings there is after dinner entertainment in the main lodge.

For Kids

Lone Mountain Ranch is a great place for children. They have a wonderful opportunity to be physically active while experiencing nature at its finest. During the summer season there is a children's program designed for children six to twelve years old. Special activities such as overnight campouts, cookouts, kids rides, rodeos, and nature walks are all part of the ranch experience. There are also some organized activities for children ages two through five, and a few afternoons a week of group babysitting.

Ages: 2-5 years old, and 6-12 years old.

Days: Daily except Sunday.

Hours: Depends on the daily schedule.

Cost: Complimentary, except for some day trips which have a small fee.

Area Attractions

Yellowstone National Park is less than an hour from the ranch. Naturalist guided all day tours are available. Lewis and Clark Caverns, Quake Lake, ghost towns, the Museum of the Rockies, and West Yellowstone's Playmill Summer Stock Theater are all nearby.

MOUNTAIN SKY GUEST RANCH

Address: P.O. Box 1128, Bozeman, Montana 59715

Telephone: (800) 548-3392, or (406) 587-1244

Location: The ranch is about 60 miles from the Bozeman Airport. Transportation to the ranch from the airport is available at an additional charge, or rental cars are available.

Lodging: Two room cabins, or three and four bedroom cabins are available, all with refrigerators.

Rates: $$$$$ Rates are weekly, Full American Plan, and include all meals, activities, and the use of the horses.

For Parents

Mountain Sky Guest Ranch is located in the beautiful and rugged Rocky Mountains close to Yellowstone National Park. Cabins, some with a fireplace, are strategically located to take full advantage of the breathtaking mountain views or carefully nestled in the pines to create a cozy setting. Your own special horse, matched to your riding ability, will be saddled and waiting for you each day. Explore miles of high country trails, or just mosey around the ranch if that suits you better. Terrific trout fishing and hiking will call to you, as well as all the tennis, swimming, horseshoes, or volleyball you could wish for. Delicious meals are served in the stunningly rustic dining room in the main lodge. Breakfast and lunch have many choices, and dinner may vary from sit-down gourmet to trailside cookouts and barbecues. There is a cocktail lounge in the main lodge. After dinner you may choose to take part in western dance instruction, volleyball and softball games, or listen to a variety of musical entertainment. Try the hot tub before bed, and you'll sleep like a baby. You will definitely not be roughing it at this guest ranch.

For Kids

A highly qualified staff is on hand to lead kids in many activities. Morning and afternoon sessions for seven to twelve year olds offer crafts, nature walks, swimming, games, and fishing in the private trout pond. Depending on the child's interest, a wrangler is on hand to take the children on trail rides or give guidance and instruction on riding. Young children three to five years old are led on horses, enjoy arts and crafts projects, and play in the playground. Younger children are also taken care of and played with. Evening activities for all age groups may include dining early on their favorite foods at a special kids dinner followed by activities like a hayride, an Indian pow-wow, or a softball game. For teens, along with the trail rides there is an unsupervised game room with ping-pong, a juke box, and a pool table.

Ages: Infant through Teen.

Days: June through mid October.

Hours: 9:00 a.m. to 8:00 p.m.

Cost: Complimentary.

Area Attractions

Yellowstone National Park is less than 30 minutes from the ranch. Naturalist guided all day tours are available there. Lewis and Clark Caverns, Quake Lake, ghost towns, the Museum of the Rockies, and West Yellowstone's Playmill Summer Stock Theater are all nearby.

PARADISE GUEST RANCH

Address: P.O. Box 790, Buffalo, Wyoming 82834

Telephone: (307) 684-7876

Location: Commuter airlines fly between Denver and Sheridan, Wyoming, which is 33 miles from the ranch. Ranch staff will be happy to pick you up, or rental cars are available there.

Lodging: A total of 18 one, two, and three bedroom cabins are available, all with fireplaces and kitchens.

Rates: $$$ Rates are weekly, Full American Plan, and include all meals, activities, and the use of the horses.

For Parents

At 7,600 feet above sea level, Paradise Ranch rests in its own mountain valley alongside French and Three Rivers creeks, a setting offering both breathtaking beauty and tranquility. The cabins are new or recently remodeled, and are clustered in an area near the main lodge. The ranch offers a flexible riding program, from one hour walking rides to all day rides with lunch packed on a mule and cooked along the trail. The programs are structured to suit your ability and interest. Besides the riding, nearby mountain lakes offer excellent trout fishing. A heated swimming pool and whirlpool spa are located at the main lodge. Other on-site activities include ping-pong and pool tables, volleyball and badminton courts, and horseshoes. Hiking and guided nature walks are very popular, and on Saturday afternoons there is a rodeo in which you can participate if the spirit moves you. In the evening there are usually slide shows, square dances, or an entertainment night. Cocktails are available in the main lodge in the French Creek Saloon.

For Kids

A special counselor coordinates activities for children under six. There is a "kiddie corral" with swings, a sandbox, and a playhouse. They will also have arts and crafts projects to enjoy. Children over six can participate in the riding program, riding the trails with wranglers. A kid's wrangler also supervises a part-time program for children six and up which has lively games like capture the flag, scavenger hunts, and creative arts and crafts projects. Swimming and hiking are always part of a day's activities. One night a week is "Kids Night Out," a camping overnight enjoyed by all. Teens at the ranch do a lot of riding and fishing and socializing with the other teen wranglers. A number of family events in the evenings are enjoyed by all ages.

Ages: 6 and up, with some activities for younger children.

Days: Monday through Saturday during the summer months.

Hours: 8:30 a.m. to 5:00 p.m.

Cost: Complimentary.

Area Attractions

Although not exactly nearby, Yellowstone National Park is about a seven hour drive west, and Mount Rushmore is about a five hour drive east.

PEACEFUL VALLEY LODGE AND RANCH

Address: Star Route, Lyons, Colorado 80540

Telephone: (303) 747-2881

Location: Peaceful Valley is located 60 miles northwest of the Denver airport. Rental cars are available, and the ranch limousine provides pickup for a fee from the air, bus, and train terminals.

Lodging: The Swiss chalet-style main lodge has two floors of rooms, and cabins continue the theme. Accommodation is offered in three rate categories: best, superior, or moderate.

Rates: $$ Full American Plan, rates are weekly, include all meals, activities, and use of the horses.

For Parents

Surrounded by the beautiful Rocky Mountains, Peaceful Valley Lodge combines the architecture of the Alps with western American ranch life. The owners are natives of Austria and Kentucky, and it is reflected in the charm and uniqueness of the ranch. In summer, horseback activities abound. Trail rides vary in length from two hours to overnights. In addition, hiking and climbing in the back country, swimming in the solar heated indoor pool, or relaxing in the whirlpool spa are all available. Tennis courts, volleyball, and horseshoes areas are all available. Trout fishing in the Rockies is famous. There is fishing on Peaceful Valley property in the Middle St. Vrain Creek, or there are nearby mountain lakes to try. In winter, Peaceful Valley transforms into a ski touring center, with miles of cross country trails. Meals are served in the main lodge in an informal setting. In the summer evenings there may be square, folk, or other dance parties, a weekly talent show, and some evenings, a sing-along.

58

For Kids
Rocky Mountain

In the summer months there is a full-time trained counselor on duty most of the day for each of four age groups. Very young children enjoy pony rides, wagon and pony cart rides, or playing with baby animals on the petting farm. For children six and older the program is active and creative, and includes daily riding instruction, hayrides, swimming, crafts, singing, sports, picnic lunches, nature lore, and hikes. Teens stay busy with more advanced horseback rides, hiking, jeep rides, dances, fireside sing-a-longs, and special outings. On Sunday evenings, there is a teens get-acquainted party. In addition, the children and the teens enjoy preparing and performing a skit or two at the weekly talent show.

Ages: 3-5 years old, 6-9 years old, 10-11 years old, and teens (12 and up).

Days: Sunday evenings to noon on Saturday.

Hours: Breakfast through supper.

Cost: Complimentary.

Area Attractions

Central City is an old mining town with historic buildings and many shops. Play golf at nearby Estes Park, take a tour through Rocky Mountain National Park, or whitewater raft on the Colorado or Poudre Rivers.

TUMBLING RIVER RANCH

Address: Grant, Colorado 80448

Telephone: (303) 838-5981

Location: Tumbling River Ranch is located about 50 miles southwest of Denver. Transportation to the ranch can be arranged, or rental cars are available.

Lodging: Accommodation is in both guest rooms and cabins.

Rates: $$$$ Rates are weekly, Full American Plan, and include all meals, activities, and use of the horses.

For Parents

Tumbling River Ranch is surrounded by Pike's Peak National Forest, boasting many of the highest peaks in the Rockies. The ranch itself is set amidst beautiful pines and aspens at 9,200 feet. Built in two clusters, the first contains the main lodge and six cabins, and the second has the Pueblo with accommodations for 16 people. There is a broad selection of activities for you to enjoy. Horseback riding, jeep trips, rafting, fishing, hiking, climbing, and swimming are all available. The ranch has a string of horses to be proud of, and they can match the capability of almost any rider with just the right horse. Each visit begins with a basic riding orientation, and all trail rides are accompanied by an experienced wrangler. When you have had your fill of vigorous activity, Tumbling River Ranch has a heated pool surrounded by glass partitions to screen you from the mountain breezes. Adjacent to the pool is a relaxing whirlpool spa, a favorite place for saddle-weary guests in the late afternoon. Evening activities include hayrides, square dancing, campfires, and cookouts. A rodeo is held the last day of your stay, and participation by both parents and kids is encouraged.

For Kids

The counselors at Tumbling River Ranch are all young, enthusiastic college kids. With separate activities for those three to five, six to eleven, and for teens, there are pony rides, trail rides (for those over five), nature hikes, fishing, swimming, hiking, or rodeo practice. A highlight of the kid's program is a trip to Silver Plume where they may ride an old narrow gauge train. For teens, the most memorable experience often is climbing up Flag Mountain and viewing the ranch and valley below. On two evenings, the children are treated to a cookout while their parents enjoy a candlelight dinner.

Ages: 3-5 years old, 6-11 years old, and teens.

Days: Tuesday through Friday during the summer months.

Hours: 9:00 a.m. to 6:30 p.m.

Cost: Complimentary.

Area Attractions

Visiting ghost towns, hiking and climbing in the Pike National Forest, picnicking, and fishing are all nearby and fun to do.

WILDERNESS TRAILS RANCH

Address: 23486 County Road 501, Bayfield, Colorado
               81122

Telephone: (303) 247-0722

Location: Wilderness Trails Ranch is about 35 miles north-
               east of Durango. The ranch staff provides trans-
               portation.

Lodging: Two, three, or five bedroom log cabins are
               available, and accommodate approximately 55
               guests each week.

Rates: $$$ Rates are weekly, Full American Plan, and
               include all meals, activities and use of the horses.

For Parents

Wilderness Trails Ranch is high up in beautiful southwest
Colorado (7,600 feet elevation), next door to the State's
largest wilderness area, the Weminuche. The picturesque
cabins are nestled among tall, fragrant spruce, pine, and aspen
trees. This ranch has horses, horses, and more horses —
enough to suit every rider's ability and experience. Riders are
divided into small groups to explore the surrounding country-
side on daily guided trail rides. Riding instruction, family
rides, and a for-real cattle round-up the last week of September
are main features of a visit to this working ranch. Wilderness
Trails breeds, raises, and trains Morgan horses, and you are
invited to hang around the corral to watch the training if you
wish. In addition there is volleyball, fishing in the ranch pond
for Rainbow trout, and even water skiing at nearby Vallecito
Lake. Delicious meals are served in the main lodge or at cook-
outs. In the evening, square dancing, a staff show, or a
campfire and sing-along under the stars can be enjoyed by the
whole family.

For Kids

The children's program is well planned. Two to five year olds enjoy their special counselor and pony rides. There is a tree house for their exclusive use, a sandbox, and a playground. Other activities include a hayride with a marshmallow roast, hikes, picnics, and crafts. The six to eleven year olds receive daily riding instruction. They also have picnics, hayrides, crafts, games, fishing, archery, hiking, and many other activities. "Frontier Day" is for both groups who become Indians for a day, complete with headbands and warpaint. They travel to a secluded area for a cookout and tales of Indian lore. Teens have organized activities designed by teens. They have riding instruction, trail rides, all day rides, hikes, volleyball, and a hayride. During the Saturday rodeo they may perform some special quadrilles. The program's structure provides flexibility for any activity they may want to do, such as have their own barn dance, or cookouts.

Ages: 2-5 years old, 6-11 years old, and 12-17 years old.

Days: Early June to early September.

Hours: 8:00 a.m. to 7:00 p.m. The children may eat with their counselors if they wish.

Cost: Complimentary.

Area Attractions

The Mesa Verde National Park has interesting pre-historic Indian ruins and fun places to picnic. A narrow guage railroad which is particularly enjoyable for the children runs from Durango to Silverton. The resort will transport you to Durango on Fridays for a raft trip run by a local rafting company.

Southwest

THE BISHOP'S LODGE

Address: P.O. Box 2367, Santa Fe, New Mexico 87504

Telephone: (505) 983-6377

Location: The Bishop's Lodge is located at the head of the Tesuque Valley, north of Santa Fe. Amtrack stops at Lamy Junction 20 miles from Santa Fe, and major airline service is available at Albuquerque International Airport. Arrangements can be made for pick up in Albuquerque.

Lodging: The Bishop's Lodge offers a variety of rooms ranging from standard rooms to deluxe suites.

Rates: $$ European Plan and Modified American Plan are offered, but European Plan is not available in July and August. (MAP includes two meals a day; EP includes none.)

For Parents

The Bishop's Lodge is horseback riders heaven, and more besides. Experienced wranglers guide you on trail rides after first making sure that you are assigned the right horse to match your experience and confidence level. Scenic foothill trails and ridges of the beautiful Sangre de Cristos provide dramatic mountain rides. A highlight of the summer season is the weekly breakfast trail ride where you rise with the sun, explore the country side, and enjoy a delicious chuckwagon breakfast. For others, golfers have playing privileges at the nearby Santa Fe and Los Alamos Country Clubs, and also at the Cochiti Lake course. Tennis buffs congregate at the four tournament-grade courts for lessons with the resident pro or round-robin mixers. Skeet and trap shooting with private instruction are available at the lodge's range. For those on MAP, breakfast and dinner are served in the main dining room; for EP, there are several good restaurants in the area.

For Kids

Trained counselors supervise children in a well-planned day camp atmosphere. Facilities and activities for teenagers are also available. Counselors and kids enjoy their meal times in the special children's dining room. Daily activities may include riding, swimming, tennis, fishing in the well stocked children's pond, hiking, arts and crafts, and lots of games. Children eight and over are welcome to join the daily trail rides. For kids seven and under there are daily arena rides. Children's tennis lesson participants are called "Shorty Swatters," and receive sound fundamentals while having fun with their peers. During each week there are special events like a cookout, bingo, a scavenger hunt, and campfire night.

Ages: 4-12 years old.

Days: June, July, and August, and during the Christmas school holiday.

Hours: 8:00 a.m. to 4:00 p.m., and 6:00 p.m. to 9:00 p.m. for dinner and evening activities.

Cost: To guests on the Modified American Plan there is no charge. There is a small charge for those on European Plan.

Area Attractions

All of the wonderful western art galleries, quaint shops, and fine restaurants of the Santa Fe area are minutes away. The open air performances of the Santa Fe Summer Opera are a special treat.

FLYING L GUEST RANCH

Address: HCR 1, Box 32, Bandera, Texas 78003

Telephone: (800) 292-5134, or (512) 796-3001

Location: The Flying L Ranch is 40 miles N.W. of San Antonio. Rental cars are available at the airport. Private aircraft may also fly into the ranch's airfield (3,250 foot runway, lighted from dusk to midnight).

Lodging: Guest accommodations are all comfortable and spacious. Each of the 38 guest houses has two rooms, a private bath, and a refrigerator.

Rates: $$ Modified American Plan, includes two meals a day, activities, and the use of the horses.

For Parents

Morning begins with fresh juice and hot coffee delivered right to your door. Then there are horseback rides on miles and miles of private scenic trails on a horse just suited to your experience (or lack of it!), an 18-hole golf course, a large heated outdoor pool, lighted tennis courts, and the nearby town of Bandera to explore. Bandera has long been considered the Cowboy Capital of the World, and is very much like the Old West used to be. Food at the Flying L is another Old West great experience. There will always be at least one Texas-style barbecue with pit-smoked brisket and chicken, and a Fiesta Mexicana with a lavish selection of traditional Tex/Mex taste tempters, or a cookout along the creek. From Memorial Day to Labor Day the Flying L puts on nightly entertainment from musical variety shows, hayrides, softball games, square dancing, hoe-downs, country-western dancing, to amazing performances by a snake handler and expert trick roper.

For Kids

The children's supervisor at The Flying L takes the kids to romp and stomp on the ranch and have a great western experience. Creekside fishing, calf roping, arts and crafts, scavenger hunts, mini-Olympics, pony rides, swimming, and playing on the new "Big Toy" playground equipment are all part of the activities offered at the ranch. For less active sports there are children's movies, board games, and a bus ride to see dinosaur tracks.

Ages: 4-10 years old, depending on the activity.

Days: The summer season is mid-May through mid-September, and also on some school holidays and other prearranged times.

Hours: 9:00 a.m.to 12:00 noon and 1:30 p.m.to 5:30 p.m.

Cost: Complimentary.

Area Attractions

Short trips that children enjoy are the Frontier Museum in Bandera, dinosaur tracks at a creek bed in Tarpley, Medina Lake for boating and fishing, and Sea World (45 minutes away in San Antonio).

Marriott's Camelback Inn

Address: 5402 E. Lincoln Drive, Scottsdale, Arizona 85253

Telephone: (800) 242-2635, or (602) 948-1700

Location: Camelback Inn is 12 miles northeast of the Phoenix Sky Harbor Airport in Paradise Valley. A commercial shuttle service is provided, or rental cars are available at the airport.

Lodging: Camelback offers pueblo styled casitas and suites. Seven suites have private pools. All rooms have private patios and refrigerators.

Rates: $

For Parents

Nestled in a valley of lush greenery and wild desert flowers, overlooked by the majestic mountain that inspired its name, Camelback's manicured lawns are punctuated by spectacular gardens and ageless saguaro cactus. Here you may choose from a wide variety of activities. The resort has two 18-hole championship golf courses, practice greens, a pro shop and a driving range. If you prefer tennis, ten tennis courts, five illuminated for night, await your pleasure. And for those who enjoy more leisurely activities, there are three outdoor swimming pools, Jacuzzi spas, table tennis, shuffleboard, a 9-hole three-par pitch and putt course, bicycle rentals, and hiking trails. The resort also contains a 25,000 square foot world-class European Health Spa with all the amenities. In Scottsdale, an assortment of beautiful boutiques, art galleries, and fine restaurants are worth visiting. When dining at the resort you can choose anything from the Sprouts Health Eatery to the Chaparral Dining Room serving the finest in continental cuisine. If you are ready for more, dancing and live entertainment swing into action nightly at the Chaparral Lounge.

For Kids

Camelback Inn's Hopalong College is supervised by trained staff, and the ratio of child to counselor varies from 5:1 to 10:1. There are two children's sessions offered each day, as well as a teen program in the evening. Children choose from a variety of activities each day which are often centered around the theme for the day. The mainstay of the program includes tennis, swimming, playground activities, and other outdoor fun. In the evening, activities vary from arts and crafts to special theme activities.

Ages: 5-12 years old and teens.

Days: Hopalong College is offered at Thanksgiving, Christmas, Easter, and during the summer on weekends from Memorial day through Labor day.

Hours: 9:00 a.m. to 12:00 noon, and 5:30 p.m. to 9:00 p.m. The teen program also runs from 5:30 p.m. to 9:00 p.m.

Cost: The cost for the morning session is $10.00 per child, and includes lunch. The evening session costs $11.50 per child, and includes dinner. The teen program is $5.00 per teen.

Area Attractions

Cave Creek is an authentic looking Western town near Carefree. Rawhide, Arizona's 1810 town, still has dirt streets, boardwalks, and original buildings. The McCormick Railroad Park has train rides, a playground, and spaces for picnicking. Old Scottsdale is a shoppers delight with over 150 galleries, boutiques, and restaurants.

SHERATON EL CONQUISTADOR RESORT

Address: 10000 N. Oracle Rd., Tucson, Arizona 85737

Telephone: (800) 325-7832, or (602) 742-7000

Location: The El Conquistador is 45 minutes from the Tucson International Airport. Rental cars are available

Lodging: 440 guest rooms and one- or two-bedroom casita suites with fireplaces are offered, all with refrigerators and mini-bars.

Rates: $ Summer packages are available. Kids six and under eat free at every meal.

For Parents

The Sheraton El Conquistador is surrounded by a spectacular desert setting with sheer granite cliffs rising in the background. The 320 acre resort is the site of 45 holes of championship golf, a driving range, and two pro shops. Because the golf courses encircle the resort, there is a feeling of lush greenery all about. But this resort is not just golf. For tennis there are 15 lighted courts at the Club and 16 more at the resort. Private and group lessons are available, as are junior and adult player programs. As part of the exercise facility there are daily aerobics and aqua-aerobics classes. Eight racquetball courts, and several swimming pools and spas are scattered throughout the complex, several near the casitas. The main pool is a NCAA size, six-lane pool, which is great for swimming laps. Dining at El Conquistador can be as casual or elegant as you are in the mood for. One restaurant, separate from the main building, is called The Last Territory. It is great for family dinners, and comes complete with stagecoach, country-western band, and an old time General Store.

For Kids

The Sheraton Tucson El Conquistador offers several camps for your child to choose from during the summer months. The day camp at the Country Club is for children six to twelve years old. Their goal for the camp is to provide children with a fun filled, creative growth experience, in a sports oriented atmosphere. Racquetball, tennis, swimming, arts and crafts, and relay games are among the offerings. Children may attend either a full day or half day session. If your child would enjoy a tennis or basketball camp, the resort offers that as well. The camps are run by Don Dickinson, Director of Tennis, and are for children from Grade 3 to Grade 8. The resort can give you exact times and dates. Camp Conquistador is the complimentary children's program. This program is held at the resort (rather than the Country Club). There are pool and courtyard games in the morning. After a break for lunch with parents, children enjoy arts and crafts, tye-dyeing, or a nature walk, followed by a movie.

Ages: 6-12 years old except for the sports camps.

Days: Monday - Saturday from early June to early September for Camp Conquistador. Monday - Friday for the Country Club camp.

Hours: 9:30 a.m. to 4:30 p.m. for Camp Conquistador, 7:30 a.m. to 3:00 p.m. for the Country Club camp.

Cost: Camp Conquistador is complimentary. The Country Club camp is $17.50 for a full day and $9.00 for a half day (snack and lunch provided).

Area Attractions

(See The Westin La Paloma)

THE WESTIN LA PALOMA

Address: 3800 East Sunrise Drive, Tucson, Arizona 85718

Telephone: (800) 876-3683, or (602) 742-6000

Location: The Westin La Paloma is located 20 minutes north of the Tucson International Airport. Rental cars are available at both the airport and the resort.

Lodging: Single and double deluxe rooms and some suites are offered.

Rates: $$

For Parents

Nestled in the beautiful rolling foothills of north Tucson, The Westin La Paloma provides an elegant setting for a desert vacation. Within the resort, a wide variety of activities await you. Jack Nicklaus personally designed the challenging 27-hole golf course, and it has been named one of the ten best courses in Arizona. A full range of additional activities complement the golf course. Twelve competition-caliber tennis courts (four clay) ensure you will be able to get a court when you want one, and there is a complete pro shop and a teaching pro. A free-form swimming pool with waterslide and swim-up bar are fun in the sun, and there are Jacuzzi spas, a sandy beach area with a volleyball court, a croquet area, ping-pong, and extensive jogging and cycling trails. A fully-equipped health club features an on-going selection of aerobics classes, and the latest Nautilus equipment is available in the weight room. For dining, La Paloma offers four great options. Sabinos (swim-up bar and grill), Sprouts (healthful snack bar), the Desert Garden for casual dining, and La Villa for fresh fish and seafood. In the evening, dance to hits of the 50's, 60's, 70's, and 80's while enjoying a panoramic view of the sparkling city lights of Tucson.

74

For Kids

During the summer season (end of May through the first of September), La Paloma offers a children's camp. The camp has a well planned schedule of activities for children five to twelve years of age. Each day is different throughout the course of a week so that children who participate for several days do not experience the same line-up of activities twice. A day may include youth aerobics, water sports, arts and crafts, and table tennis matches. Junior sports clinics are available on weekends, as well as on week days during the summer. They include golf and tennis seminars given by La Paloma staff pros. The weekend clinics begin at 8:00 a.m. and run until noon. The weekday clinics also begin at 8:00 a.m., but run until 2:00 p.m. with a break for lunch. The cost of the clinics is $5.00 per child per hour, or children can participate in the full clinic for a discounted price of $10.00 for the weekend clinics and $20.00 for the weekday clinics. Weekday clinics include lunch.

Ages: 5-12 years old.

Days: Monday through Saturday from May to September.

Hours: 10:00 a.m. to 3:00 p.m.

Cost: $20.00 per child (includes lunch).

Area Attractions

Try Sabino Canyon with a picnic lunch. Old Tucson Movie Studios, The Arizona-Sonora Desert Museum, and San Xavier Mission are also wonderful. For a full day trip, explore the old mining towns of Bisbee and Tombstone (where the shoot-out at the OK Corral took place).

THE WICKENBURG INN

Address: P.O. Box P, Wickenburg, Arizona 85358

Telephone: (800) 528-4277, or (602) 684-7811

Location: The Wickenburg Inn is eight miles north of Wickenburg, Arizona, on Route 89, a 70 mile drive northwest from Phoenix on I-17. Rental cars are available from either the Phoenix or Wickenburg airports.

Lodging: Spanish-style adobe casitas or ranch-style lodge rooms are available. Casitas include fireplaces and wet bars.

Rates: $ Rates are Full American Plan and include all meals.

For Parents

If you are on the lookout for an out-of-the-way resort and tennis camp in a unique environment, the Wickenburg Inn may be just the place for you. The inn offers tennis, horseback riding, nature study, and arts and crafts in a spectacular western ranch setting. Tennis instruction and clinics are offered on 11 acrylic courts nestled in a low, wind-protected valley oriented away from the sun's glare. Horseback riding is an adventure not to be missed. Dozens of riding trails wind through a display of vibrant desert scenery. You will enjoy guided trail rides conducted by knowledgeable wranglers, on a horse to suit your experience. At the inn's arts and crafts center, let your creative imagination flow. Sketching, painting, pottery, leather work, macrame, and weaving are available. Of course there's swimming, a hill top spa, and a sun deck. A delicious assortment of continental and southwestern specialities await diners. Menus feature home style soups, breads and pastries, and the western steak fry and sing-along under the stars will bring out the wrangler in you.

For Kids

The Wickenburg Inn's children's program is under the supervision of qualified counselors and is divided into three age groupings. While in the program, children may take advantage of all the activities the ranch has to offer; like horseback riding, tennis, archery, arts and crafts, swimming, nature hikes, and rodeos. A special kid's dinner is held at 5:00 p.m., and children may elect to eat with their counselors then or later with their parents at the regular dinner hour. There is an evening program that usually includes a movie, a game, or a campfire at Squirrel Banks.

Ages: 4-12 years old.

Days: Thanksgiving weekend (Thursday through Sunday), two weeks during the Christmas school break, and the last two weeks in March and first two weeks in April coinciding with Spring school breaks.

Hours: 9:00 a.m. to 4:00 p.m. with a break for lunch with their parents if they wish, and 6:00 p.m. to 8:00 p.m.

Cost: Full day plus evening program is $30.00 per day per child; full day program only is $25.00 per day per child.

Area Attractions

Nearby, Congress and Yarnell are great "old west" towns to visit for antiquing, art galleries, and beautiful scenery. In the hills about 75 miles away is the old mining town of Jerome. If you have the time or are heading to the Grand Canyon, Jerome is a particularly interesting town to visit.

Midwest

ARROWWOOD - A RADISSON RESORT

Address: P. O. Box 639, Alexandria, Minnesota 56038

Telephone: (612) 762-1124

Location: Arrowwood is located on Lake Darling, 130 miles northwest of the Twin Cities. Airport transportation service is available Monday through Saturday from the Minneapolis/St. Paul International Airport for a reasonable fee.

Lodging: There are 170 hotel rooms and suites. Recently renovated, most feature a lake view and a private balcony.

Rates: $$$

For Parents

Arrowwood is situated on the shores of Lake Darling. Although small in number of rooms for a resort, it occupies over 400 acres of land, giving the feeling of vast spaciousness. Summer recreation facilities feature an 18-hole golf course, four Lay-kold tennis courts, and a full marina that rents sailboats, canoes, fishing boats, speedboats, party pontoons, and paddlebikes. There is a 30-horse stable for trail rides, and there are indoor and outdoor swimming lap pools, a sauna, and a whirlpool spa. Start your day with an aerobic or aquacise workout, or take a ride on a tandem bicycle. Try your hand at archery, volleyball, or shuffleboard, or book a moonlight cruise. In winter, Arrowwood has miles of cross-country ski trails and snowmobile paths. Sleigh rides behind Belgian draft horses are fun for everyone, or ice skate on the pond. An assortment of dining alternatives are available. Swedish and North American favorites are served in the Lake Cafe overlooking Lake Darling, or pizza and ice cream can be enjoyed at Luigi's. In summer there is a pool-side bar and grill offering light snacks. Rafter's Lounge has nightly entertainment.

For Kids

Arrowwood has offered a fun children's activity program for over ten years. They are proud of their program, and feel they provide recreational opportunities that are educational and encourage team effort, individual development and achievement, while offering a fun atmosphere for meeting new friends. The Saddle-Up Program has stable staff in a show-and-tell program for children to learn about feeding, grooming, and saddling horses. Homemade fishing poles and straw hats are part of Huck Finn Fishing, whether fish are biting off the end of the dock or from a raft. There are nature walks through the woods, arts and crafts projects, paddleboat rides, archery, kickball, swimming games, and sand castle building on the beach. There is a Super Olympics of low-key competition with ribbons for everyone. Each Camp Arrowwood participant receives a Rory Raccoon Camp Arrowwood cap, and a Rory Raccoon button with his or her name on it. A picnic lunch is included in the program.

Ages: 4-12 years old, and activities for teens as needed.

Days: Daily from Memorial Day to Labor Day. Saturday only from Labor Day to Memorial Day.

Hours: 9:00 a.m. to 3:00 p.m.

Cost: $8.50 per child per day.

Area Attractions

The Kensington-Runestone Museum and Fort Alexanderia is a wonderful place to visit. It has a blacksmith shop, an old school house and a caboose that children love. Equally enjoyable is the Alexanderia Mini-Golf, Go-Carts & Batting Cages Park. For Mom, there are several antique and craft shops in the area.

EAGLE RIDGE INN & RESORT

Address: Box 777, Galena, Illinois 61036

Telephone: (800) 323-8421, or in Illinois (800) 892-2269

Location: The resort is about 3 hours from Chicago, Illinois. Nearby Dubuque, Iowa, has daily air service. Transportation by inn vehicle for the 30 mile drive can be arranged with advance notice.

Lodging: Eagle Ridge Inn offers hotel rooms in the inn, and privately owned one to four bedroom homes located throughout the property. All resort homes have fully equipped kitchens and fireplaces.

Rates: $$

For Parents

Eagle Ridge Inn is perched high on a bluff above a beautiful and serene lake, surrounded by forest and inviting green fairways. The architecture of the surrounding community ranges from New England saltbox to contemporary. Golf is the central activity at Eagle Ridge in the summer, with two 18-hole courses that rival the best in the country. In addition, a full service pro shop is ready and waiting to provide group or private lessons, and there is a large practice fairway and green. You will find tennis courts for play or for instruction, horseback riding, sail boat rentals, miles of jogging trails, and swimming in the lake or in the pool. You can fish in the lake, or simply spend the day relaxing in the sun. In winter there are over 60 kilometers of groomed cross-country ski trails at Eagle Ridge, and a cozy fireside to warm you up when you return to the lodge. There are charming outdoor and indoor restaurants at the inn and in the surrounding area serving a variety of cuisine in settings from casual to elegant.

For Kids

The children's programs are fully supervised with a low ratio of children per counselor. Children are entertained with activities such as arts and crafts, swimming, boat rides, fishing, nature walks, treasure hunts, relay games, face painting, and pony rides. The Kid's Night Out theme night is filled with fun. Themes range from Pirates of the Caribbean to Carnival Night. The evening includes dinner, party games, movies, and some outdoor activities. Teen's Night Out is a program designed with activities such as boating, cross-country and downhill skiing, horse trail rides, miniature golf, volleyball and waterpark adventures. Dinner is included in the evening functions.

Ages: 3-12 years old, and 13-19 years old.

Days: Monday through Saturday, Memorial Day through Labor Day, and major holiday weekends.

Hours: 9:00 a.m. to 1:00 p.m., and 1:00 p.m. to 4:00 p.m. for the day program. The evening program is 7:00 p.m. to 10:00 p.m.

Cost: Morning session, $15.00 (lunch included). Afternoon session, $13.00. Full day session, $18.00 (lunch included). Teen program fees and evening session fees vary with the activities.

Area Attractions

Seven miles down the road is charming, historic Galena, Illinois, "the town time forgot." Once home of lead mines, paddlewheelers, and General Grant, Galena is an enchanting old town that gives you a glimpse of 19th century life.

FRENCH LICK SPRINGS RESORT

Address: French Lick, Indiana 47432

Telephone: (800) 742-4095, or (812) 936-9300

Location: In southwestern Indiana, French Lick Springs is about 75 miles from the Louisville, Kentucky Airport. Rental cars are available.

Lodging: There are 485 hotel rooms in one main building, and a few more in annexes, many recently re-decorated. Suites with adjacent sitting rooms are available. This hotel was built in the early 1900's, but has been updated, refurbished, and well-maintained since that time.

Rates: $$ Modified American Plan.

For Parents

French Lick Springs is in an area in the Cumberland hills where mineral springs have been used for more than 150 years as a spa. But the attraction is no longer just the "miracle waters." This resort is one of the most extensive in the Midwest. Eighteen lighted tennis courts (8 indoor and 10 outdoor) mean a court is usually available when you want one. Two 18-hole golf courses offer different challenges, and a lighted driving range assures plenty of time to practice. An indoor-outdoor swimming pool with retractable dome, and an Olympic-sized outdoor pool with a shallow end offer swimming for the whole family. A riding stable with guided trail rides, boat rentals, fishing expeditions, and a recreation center with health spa and gym means there is something for everyone. On-site are four restaurants, a pizzeria, and an ice cream parlor. The Hoosier Rib Room, the resort's main dining room, requires that men wear jackets at dinner. The Bistro offers live entertainment Wednesdays through Sundays.

For Kids

The new Pluto Club for children is divided into age groupings, and changes regularly to allow kids to participate in a variety of athletic, recreational, and creative activities. A well-trained staff plan and run daily theme events in the summer to allow Pluto Club kids to learn about a range of subjects from the wild west to African safaris. Activities may include crafts, hikes, cookouts, pool events, parachute games, films, hayrides, and more. For teens there are mini-golf tournaments, horseback rides, and scavenger hunts. There are also junior tennis and golf clinics that children can attend on their own.

Ages: 3-5 years old, 6-12 years old, and 12 and over.

Days: Seven days a week from Memorial Day through Labor Day with programs for 5-12 year olds every Saturday throughout the year. Both day and evening programs are offered during holidays.

Hours: 9:00 a.m. to 5:00 p.m. (includes lunch).

Cost: $8.00 per child per day. Lunch is an additional charge.

Area Attractions

There are many antique shops in the area for the antique buff. The Children's Museum of Indianapolis is the largest and one of the best hands-on children's museums in the world. It is well worth the 90 minute drive.

GRAND VIEW LODGE

Address: South 134 Nokomis, Nisswa, Minnesota 56468

Telephone: (218) 963-2234

Location: Grand View Lodge is 142 miles northwest of Minneapolis, and 120 miles west of Duluth. Private planes may use Brainerd Airport.

Lodging: There is a main building with 14 rooms, and 60 cottages ranging in size from one bedroom to eight bedrooms. Some have kitchenettes.

Rates: $$$ Modified American Plan, includes breakfast and lunch and use of most facilities.

For Parents

Grand View Lodge is a small family owned resort on Gull Lake. The lodge was selected for the National Register of Historic Places in 1979 as an exceptionally preserved example of log resort architecture dating to the early 1900's. You may enjoy unlimited golf and tennis here, as well as use of nonmotorized fishing boats, canoes, and kayaks. The tennis program includes 11 Lay-kold courts, free children's tennis clinics, and a pro who conducts group mixers and gives private lessons. Tournaments are held Memorial Day, Labor Day and on some weekends throughout the summer. For water enthusiasts, fifteen hundred feet of natural sandy beach is complemented by a heated indoor/outdoor pool and Jacuzzi whirlpool, saunas, and an exercise room. There are sailboats, waterski boats and equipment for rent. A sunken island offshore is a prime walleye fishing spot, with fish in the 8-12 pound category. The lake itself is large enough to accommodate motor boating, and exploring the seven lake chain connecting into Gull lake is fun. There are three dining rooms at Grand View featuring a variety of cuisine, and the cocktail lounge regularly schedules live music and dances.

For Kids

The children's program at Grandview Lodge offers exciting and unique activities for children from morning till bedtime if they wish. Three full-time youth counselors supervise the activities. Broken into three daily sessions, activities include arts and crafts, sand castle building, relay races, hay rides, nature walks, a children's talent show, and beach and pool activities. In addition, story telling, ball games, or time on playground equipment are usually part of the day's activities.

Ages: 3-12 years old.

Days: Monday through Saturday from the beginning of May through the end of August.

Hours: 9:30 a.m. to 12:00 noon for ages 3-12; 1:30 p.m. to 3:30 p.m. for ages 6-12. The evening session is for all ages, and runs from 5:30 p.m. to 8:00 p.m.

Cost: Complimentary.

Area Attractions

The Paul Bunyan amusement center, Deep Portage Nature Reserve, Deer Park Zoo, the Funland Center and Nisswa Lakes Plaza are all near.

THE LODGE OF FOUR SEASONS

Address: Lake Road HH, Lake Ozark, Missouri 65049

Telephone: (800) The Lake, or (314) 365-3000.

Location: Along the Lake of the Ozarks on Highway 54, midway between St. Louis and Kansas City, Missouri airports.

Lodging: There are 311 rooms and suites, plus condominium rentals of one, two, and three bedroom privately owned villas.

Rates: $$ Several packages are available.

For Parents

Tucked into the rolling hills of the Ozark Mountains and surrounded by beautiful Lake of the Ozarks is The Lodge Of Four Seasons. The resort which began two decades ago as a lodge is now a community of vacation homes, year around residences, and superior sporting, recreation, and health and fitness facilities. Six swimming pools, 18-hole and 9-hole golf courses, 23 tennis courts, and two racquetball courts offer plenty in the way of energetic outdoor recreation. In addition to a riding stable and volleyball and basketball courts, there are hiking, biking, and jogging trails in the summer that turn into cross-country ski trails in the winter. Trapshooting, bowling, billiards, ping-pong, sailing, and almost all water sports are a part of the recreation opportunities offered. The world-class health and fitness center features state-of-the-art exercise machines. The Racquet Club provides racquetball courts and indoor and outdoor pools. For fishermen, the Lake of the Ozarks is one of the country's prime bass fishing spots. Fishing licenses, boats, and guides are available at the Lodge. Seven on-site restaurants provide dining from Four-Star to casual in a variety of settings, and the Fifth Season nightclub has live music each evening.

For Kids

The Lodge Of Four Seasons has a youth program called The Sunshine Club. Designed to provide special meaning for every child, it includes a variety of memorable activities. Under the direction of the youth program coordinator, The Sunshine Club is also supervised by senior college interns working toward B.S. degrees in recreation. Activities may include field trips, pool parties, games, arts and crafts, boating, movies, and much more. In addition, youngsters of all ages may participate in tennis camps and junior golf programs, and join their parents for boating, skiing, horseback riding, fishing, and swimming.

Ages: 4-14 years old.

Days: Monday through Saturday.

Hours: 9:00 a.m. to 4:00 p.m., and 6:00 p.m. to 9:00 p.m.

Cost: Complimentary (except for lunch and special events).

Area Attractions

Lake of the Ozarks State Park is nearby. Tours of nearby Bagnall Dam are offered daily. There are also three caves in the area that have tours: Bridal Cave, Fantasy World Caverns, and Ozark Caverns. Osage Beach has a shopping center, factory outlet stores, and small shops with country crafts and antiques. Ha Ha Tonka State Park has some of the most beautiful scenery on the lake, as well as the picturesque ruins of an old castle.

MARRIOTT'S TAN-TAR-A RESORT

Address: Lake of the Ozarks, Osage Beach, Missouri
65065

Telephone: (800) MARRIOTT, or (314) 348-3131

Location: The resort is located about half way between St.
Louis and Kansas City. The Lee C. Fine airport
is 14 miles away.

Lodging: Tan-Tar-A has a variety of configurations ranging from cabins to suites. It includes both hotel
rooms and condominium-type accommodations
with as many as five bedrooms. (Many of the
privately owned condominiums are right on the
lakeshore.)

Rates: $$ Several packages are available.

For Parents

Tan-Tar-A occupies more than 400 acres of woods and wind-
ing trails on the shore of the beautiful Lake of the Ozarks.
Although billed as a golf resort, there are more than 25
recreational activities available. There are lighted tennis
courts (including two indoors), and racketball courts. There
is an 18-hole golf course and a 9-hole golf course, a driving
range, and a pro shop with rental equipment available. A
sandy beach on the lake invites swimming, as do the five
swimming pools (one indoor). Rental canoes, paddleboats,
sailboats, houseboats, fishing boats, and ski boats are abun-
dant. A spa with exercise equipment, aerobics classes, mas-
sages, and marked jogging trails will help you toward fitness,
and bicycles, a stable, hayrides, a bowling alley, and billiard
tables are all handy. Plays and musicals are presented regu-
larly in the resort's theater. There are six restaurants from
moderate to upscale, cocktail lounges, nightclub entertain-
ment, and more than a dozen shops on the premises.

For Kids

The recreation staff at Tan-Tar-A includes school teachers and others with recreation expertise. Playcamp is open for six hours each weekday during the summer. Youngsters may swim, create arts and crafts, play games, participate in a treasure hunt, make ice cream, or feed the fish. There is also a playroom equipped with books, blocks, toys, dress-up clothes, and television. At unsupervised Garden of Games, families can play miniature golf, bocci, and other games together. It includes a kiddie play park and a moon walk. For teens up to 17 there is a special program that includes beach volleyball, paddleboat races, and video games. A supervised children's dinner is held at the Grill Monday through Saturday during the summer and on weekends during the rest of the year.

Ages: 5-12 years old, and 12-17 years old.

Days: Monday through Friday during the summer months.

Hours: 9:30 a.m. to 3:30 p.m.

Cost: $15.00 per day per child (includes lunch). Prices vary depending on the activity for teens.

Area Attractions

Lake of the Ozarks State Park is nearby. Tours of Bagnall Dam are offered daily. There are three caves within a 25 minute drive that have tours: Bridal Cave, Fantasy World Caverns, and Ozark Caverns. Osage Beach has a shopping center, factory outlet stores, and small shops with country crafts and antiques. Ha Ha Tonka State Park has some of the most beautiful scenery on the lake, as well as the picturesque ruins of an old castle.

East

THE BALSAMS

Address: Dixville Notch, New Hampshire 03576

Telephone: (800) 255-0600, or in New Hampshire (800) 255-0800

Location: The Balsams is about 390 miles from New York, 219 miles from Boston, and 152 miles from Montreal. It is served by bus from Logan airport in Boston. Hotel transportation pick-up may also be arranged.

Lodging: Standard to deluxe rooms, along with a few family suites.

Rates: $$ Full American Plan (includes all meals and activities).

For Parents

The Balsams Grand Resort Hotel is a magnificent 15,000 acre estate high in New Hampshire's beautiful White Mountains. You will find a variety of group and individual activities from volleyball and shuffleboard to a fascinating natural history program. There is a professionally directed recreation staff responsible for organizing group activities daily. The 6804-yard championship golf course at the Panorama Golf Club was built on the western slope of Keyser Mountain. It affords spectacular views of two states and Canada, while challenging the skills of all who play it. The 9-hole Executive Course is 1,960 yards long, just right for your warm up, or for those who like a shorter course. In addition to the 27 holes of golf and six tennis courts, there are boating, swimming, fishing, hiking, bicycling, croquet, and feature length movies every day. At meal time, Chef Learned's renowned cuisine with choice-of-menu dining is sure to please every palate. Each night a variety of concerts, musical performances, and cabaret circuit performers fill three rooms of entertainment.

94

For Kids

Children between the ages of five and twelve are welcome to participate in the program conducted by a staff of adult counselors and their assistants. Children may choose to join their parents instead of the counselors for any meal during the day, and they may participate in either or both the morning and afternoon activities programs. Activities during the day are chosen from outdoor sports, picnics, swimming, treasure hunts, games, farm visits, arts and crafts, and movies. Facilities include a playroom, playground and game room with ping-pong, pin ball, and an arcade with video games. The teen club offers special events in the evenings.

Ages: 5-12 years old.

Days: Seven days a week from the 4th of July weekend through the Labor Day weekend.

Hours: 9:30 a.m.to 4:00 p.m., and 6:30 p.m.to 9:00 p.m.

Cost: Complimentary.

Area Attractions

There are a number of day trips a comfortable drive from the hotel. Attractions which appeal to children of all ages are: Granby Zoo, Storyland, and Santa's Village. For beautiful scenery, visit Franconia Notch, the Androscoggin River, or drive the Kancamagus Highway. For great nearby shopping there is Littleton, North Conway, and Sherbrooke.

BASIN HARBOR CLUB

Address: Vergennes, Vermont 05491

Telephone: (802) 475-2311

Location: Basin Harbor is a 45 minute drive from Burlington International, Vermont's largest commercial airport. There is also a 3,200 ft. grass strip for private aircraft located at Basin Harbor.

Lodging: Seventy-seven comfortably furnished guest cottages resemble private homes that sleep from two to six people. There are also 44 twin and single rooms in the Lodge, Harbor Homestead, and Champlain House.

Rates: $$ Full American Plan (includes all meals and use of most facilities).

For Parents

Basin Harbor Club is a 700-acre resort on the eastern shore of Lake Champlain. With over 600 miles of shoreline, Lake Champlain offers spectacular boating fun. The resort's harbormaster will arrange for canoes, rowboats, small outboards, Sunfish, or windsurfers, or you can enjoy a tour of the lake aboard the Dynamyte II. Swimming is equally enjoyable in the lake or in the beautiful Olympic-size pool. Tennis and golf lovers will appreciate Basin Harbor's fine facilities and professional staff. The five tennis courts include two Har-Tru and three all weather surfaces. The first tee of the scenic 18-hole golf course is right at the front door. Practice greens, chipping areas, and a driving range are all on site. There are miles of jogging and exercise trails, shuffleboard and croquet areas, and bicycles for rent. Basin Harbor's classic New England cuisine includes a hearty breakfast and bountiful buffet lunch. Dinners feature a wide range of classic entrees.

For Kids

The children's program at Basin Harbor divides participants into age groups of approximately three to five and six to twelve years old. Activities may include arts and crafts, water play, nature walks, or games. The resort has a fully-equipped playground with swings, jungle gyms, slides, a sandbox and a playhouse. Children eat lunch with either the recreation staff or their parents. In the evening, children may wish to join the recreation staff at the Kid's Table. After dinner entertainment often includes scavenger hunts, quiet games, or stories and/or videos, depending on the interests and ages of the children involved. For pre-teens and teens, junior golf and tennis clinics, picnics, canoe trips, and hikes are among the activities organized.

Ages: 3-10 years old, pre-teens, and teens.

Days: Late June to the first week of September.

Hours: 9 a.m. to 1:00 p.m., and 6:00 p.m.to 9:00 p.m.

Cost: Complimentary.

Area Attractions

You may wish to visit the nearby Lake Champlain Maritime Museum, Fort Ticonderoga, the Vermont Marble Works, Frog Hollow State Craft Center, or the Kennedy Brothers Factory Marketplace during your visit.

HAWK INN AND MOUNTAIN RESORT

Address: P. O. Box 64, Route 100, Plymouth, Vermont 05056

Telephone: (800) 451-4109, or (802) 672-3811

Location: The resort is easily accessible from the airports in Burlington and Rutland, Vermont and Lebanon, New Hampshire.

Lodging: Accommodations range from a luxurious country inn to private, custom-built homes and townhouses ranging in size from two to four bedrooms.

Rates: $$ Discounted five and seven night packages are available. Breakfast and most activities are included in the daily rate.

For Parents

The Hawk Inn and Mountain Resort is situated on 1,176 acres of unspoiled terrain in the heart of the beautiful Green Mountains. Although this is a year around resort, their children's program is in the summer, and so our focus is on the summer activities available for parents, too. The resort offers a wide variety of outdoor adventures from boating to bicycling, and everything in between. Swimming, fishing, tennis and croquet, and even an equestrian program are ready to make your stay a busy one. Hikers will enjoy the many miles of trails through the mountains, and gold panning expeditions are exciting and instructive. The resort also houses a new health spa featuring the most up-to-date exercise equipment available, a giant hot tub, and a beautiful glass-enclosed heated pool. The River Tavern, Hawk's restaurant, is a favorite throughout the region. There are wonderful views of the mountains and river from the main dining area. After dinner there are lawn concerts under the stars for the entire family.

For Kids

Hawk's Summer Adventure Program for children is now in its twelfth year. Children enjoy the delights of the Green Mountains as they hike, swim, play tennis, horseback ride, and participate in a variety of crafts, games, and special projects. The camp's philosophy is to provide the children with strong encouragement to participate, with emphasis placed on enjoyment rather than competition to win. Little Adventure is designed to please children ages three to five. Youth Adventure is for ages six to twelve years, and focuses on outdoor sports and recreation activities.

Ages: 3-12 years old.

Days: Daily during the summer months.

Hours: 10:00 a.m. to 3:00 p.m.

Cost: $5.00 per day, per child.

Area Attractions

Interesting day trips for families are the Calvin Coolidge Homestead in Plymouth, the Pico Alpine Slide and Killington Gondola Ride in Killington, and the Norman Rockwell Museum in Rutland.

PINEGROVE RESORT RANCH

Address: Lower Cherrytown Road, Kerhonkson, New York 12446

Telephone: (914) 626-7345

Location: The Ranch is 30 miles from Stewart International and 90 miles from the Newark Airport.

Lodging: Villas with one, two, or three bedrooms, kitchens and sitting rooms. Motel-style rooms are also available without kitchens.

Rates: $ Full American Plan, includes all meals and use of all facilities.

For Parents

The folks at Pinegrove believe that it is the only ranch in the world that breeds its own purebred and half-bred registered Arabian saddle horses. They have horses trained to Western and English riding that carry you over acres of picturesque mountain trails. Or, you can go deep into the forest for miles of secluded trails that take you up and down mountainsides, crossing streams, and affording breathtaking views on all sides. But there is more to do at Pinegrove than ride. The resort also offers on-site tennis, swimming, a mini golf course, a rifle range, volleyball, shuffleboard and a game room. There are three 18-hole golf courses nearby for the golfers in your party. Meals are served in the dining room overlooking the beautiful Shawangunk Mountains. For the nibbler or the real hungry wranglers, the family-style Chuck Wagon offers help yourself home cooked snacks in between meals and late at night. After dinner there is entertainment and a resident dance to band to help you while away the evening hours until you are ready to call it a day.

100

For Kids

The Children's camp at Pinegrove is designed for children from two to sixteen. Each age group is led by experienced counselors, and they supervise age-appropriate games and activities for each group. Two and three year olds may play in the playground, visit the animal petting farm, go on hay-rides, and listen to stories. Four to six year olds ride the ponies, swim, participate in outdoor games and activities, and are absorbed by interesting arts and crafts projects. Older children have horseback riding, swimming, arts and crafts, and outdoor activities. Your teenagers will enjoy the less structured program of volleyball, softball, horseback riding, disco parties, and swimming.

Ages: 2-16 years old.

Days: All year around (if you are traveling off season it would be best to check the schedule).

Hours: 10:00 a.m. to 5:00 p.m.

Cost: Complimentary.

Area Attractions

The Hudson River Cruise and Museum and the Catskill Game Farm are both fun for families.

THE PINES RESORT HOTEL

Address: South Fallsburg, New York 12779

Telephone: (800) 36-PINES, or (914) 434-6000

Location: One hundred miles north and west of New York
City. Thirty miles from Stewart International
Airport. Limousine service is available.

Lodging: Standard to super deluxe rooms are available, all
with refrigerators.

Rates: $$ Full American Plan, includes all meals and
use of facilities.

For Parents

Years ago, family resorts in the enchanting green Catskill
Mountains made their reputations as great places to get out of
the city during the heat of the summer. Now, most of the big
resort hotels are year around establishments. So too is The
Pines. During the summer months you will enjoy many fun
hours of unlimited tennis, paddleball, golf on the Sportsman
Course, swimming, or just relaxing in the sun. When the
weather turns cold and winter descends upon the mountains,
The Pines offers you ice skating, a huge heated indoor pool,
several indoor tennis courts, a sauna, a complete modern
health and fitness club, and, of course skiing. There are six
downhill ski slopes with lifts, miles of scenic winter-wonder-
land cross country trails, a thrilling-chilling toboggan run, and
exhilarating snowmobile rides. All year around The Pines
follows today's trend toward dining, which means healthier
foods and careful preparation. But don't worry, you can still
order seconds and thirds if you like, and as always you will
choose from a selection of entrees and desserts to suit every
taste. After dinner there is lively evening entertainment for the
whole family.

For Kids

Day Camp at The Pines is for children three years of age and older. Activities may include arts and crafts, basketball, board games, bowling, circle games, hayrides, kickball, miniature golf, pony rides, swimming, clowns, magic shows, and more. In summer, children under two are assigned a mother's helper at no charge; the rest of the year there is a small charge. The Pines pre-teen and teen programs are aimed entirely at activities that meet the athletic and social interests of the group. During the day, activities may include basketball, bowling, golf, horseback riding, softball, swimming, tennis, and volleyball. In the evenings there is a non-alcoholic dance club, movies, campfires, hayrides, and even late night volleyball, tennis, and basketball in the indoor tennis center.

Ages: All ages through teen.

Days: Year around.

Hours: 8:15 a.m. to 4:00 p.m., and 6:15 p.m. to 8:15 p.m.

Cost: Complimentary except for a minimal charge for pony rides and ice skating.

Area Attractions

The Catskill Game Farm with its animals and rides makes an enjoyable side trip, as do the Hudson Valley Tours and the Vanderbilt and Roosevelt Mansions in Hyde Park.

ROCKING HORSE RANCH

Address: 600 RT 44-55, Highland, New York 12528-9906

Telephone: (800) 647-2624, or (914) 691-2927.

Location: About a ten minute drive from Poughkeepsie, New York. Driving, bus, or train directions are available from the resort.

Lodging: The Oklahoma building is motel style, with couple and family sized rooms. The main lodge has standard sized rooms and king ranchettes with refrigerators and a separate sitting area.

Rates: $$ Full American Plan, includes meals and all activities. Many packages are available.

For Parents

Rocking Horse Ranch is located on 500 acres of scenic mountain and orchard land in beautiful up-state New York. At this eastern dude ranch you can spend your days around the corrals and stables getting to know the horses, or ride the miles of trails. Try your hand at target shooting out back, or take aim with a bow and arrow. Or you may want to just sit back and soak up the sun and scenery, and that's all right, too. When you are refreshed and ready to go again, there are all weather tennis courts and two swimming pools on site just waiting for you, and an 18-hole golf course nearby. In the summer months, water ski behind a fast boat or drift along in a silent canoe on the ranch's private lake. Tennis and swimming lessons are available, and water-skiing and horseback riding instruction are all offered at no additional charge, so you can learn them all or pick and choose. Dining at the ranch is a 6-7 course selection served in a large modern dining room. After dinner there is always live entertainment in the Round-Up Room nightclub.

For Kids

The day camp at Rocking Horse allows kids to experience all that is special about the ranch in a safe, supervised environment. During the day there are scavenger hunts, nature hikes, hay and buggy rides, swimming, fishing, water skiing, archery, croquet, arts and crafts, and more. For something special, there is also a petting zoo featuring a pet llama.

Ages: 6-14 years old.

Days: From Labor Day to Memorial Day and major school holidays.

Hours: 9:00 a.m. to 4:30 p.m. Children may choose to eat lunch and dinner with their parents, or with their counselors.

Cost: Complimentary.

Area Attractions

For families, there are the Roosevelt and Vanderbilt Mansions in Hyde Park, Huegenot Street in New Platz with the oldest stone houses in the U.S., and the W.W.I "Aerodrome" in Rhinebeck with staged airwars.

THE SAGAMORE

Address: Bolton Landing, New York 12814

Telephone: (800) 358-3585, or (518) 644-9400

Location: One hour from the Albany County airport. Resort shuttle service is available.

Lodging: The main hotel's 100 rooms include 46 suites. Lodges offer 240 rooms including 120 suites with fireplaces and wet bars.

Rates: $$ Modified American Plan (includes dinner and breakfast daily, a Morgan Lake cruise, and the children's program).

For Parents

The Sagamore is one of the more spectacular resorts in the Southern Adirondaks. Overlooking Lake George from its own 70-acre island, the resort is steeped in history and style. You can start out by just relaxing, but if it's action you want there's plenty of it here. On the mainland overlooking the Lake George Basin is the fully-restored Sagamore Golf Club, a par 70, 18-hole championship course designed by Donald Ross. The marina offers dockage for 78 pleasure craft. Lake activities at the resort and in the area are water-skiing, canoeing, sailing, lake cruises, parasailing, scuba diving, and windsurfing. The tennis complex has two indoor tennis courts, a racquetball court, pro shop, courtside lounge, and four all-weather outdoor courts with lights for night play. In the afternoon during high season, the hotel offers horse drawn carriage rides. The nature trail ensures joggers an exhilarating run with spectacular lake views. For dining, the resort offers styles from elegantly formal to sporty and casual. And if that isn't enough you can always drop in to VanWinkles' nightclub and boogie until the wee hours.

106

For Kids

The children's program at The Sagamore is broken into age groupings of three to five and six to thirteen year olds. Each activity is supervised by experienced, mature counselors, many with teaching credentials. For the younger children, sand and water play, arts and crafts, a movie festival, theme parties, and story hours are part of the program. For older kids, ages six to thirteen, nature exploration, outdoor games, arts and crafts, pool fun, and a movie festival are offered. Lunch and dinner are also supervised.

Ages: 3-13 years old.

Days: Seven days a week from mid-June through Labor Day. The program is also offered on all major holidays.

Hours: 9:00 a.m. to 4:00 p.m. and again from 6:00 p.m. to 9:00 p.m.

Cost: Complimentary to guests on the Family Package throughout the summer. There is a small charge other times.

Area Attractions

The Lake George area offers a wealth of family-oriented activities. Among them are the Great Escape Fun Park, Lake George Village for shopping, Water Slide World, horseback riding at Saddle Up stables, Adirondack Museum and the Hyde Museum.

SMUGGLERS' NOTCH RESORT

Address: Smugglers' Notch, Vermont 05464

Telephone: (800) 451-8752, or (802) 644-8851

Location: Thirty miles northeast of Burlington International Airport and five miles southwest of Jeffersonville. Airport and Amtrack resort shuttle service is available with advance reservations.

Lodging: Hotel and condominium-style accommodations ranging in size from one room motel type units to five bedroom condominiums.

Rates: $ Several packages are available.

For Parents

Smugglers' Notch Resort is surrounded by the beautiful Green Mountains of Vermont. The main emphasis of the resort is on family activities and on providing an abundance of activities for all ages. For grown-ups, there are two swimming pools, hot tubs, fly fishing clinics, shuffleboard, softball, horseshoes, volleyball, mountain biking, guided walks, hiking, and more. Privately owned stables adjacent to The Village offer instruction and riding adventures into the mountains. The Stowe Country Club, with an 18-hole championship golf course, welcomes Smugglers' Notch guests who pay green fees or take part in the Golfers Package. For tennis enthusiasts, qualified instructors are on hand to provide lessons and clinics. The natural waters surrounding the resort provide for other adventures and discoveries. There is excellent trout fishing in Sterling Pond, beaver watching at the reservoir, and canoeing on the Lamoille River. In the evening, you will enjoy barbecues, game nights, and bonfires. There is a country store and several additional restaurants in the Village, so dining can be either in or out at your pleasure.

For Kids

The supervised children's program at Smugglers' Notch comes complete with a "Kids' Fun Guarantee." The Discovery Day Camp for three to six year olds provides arts and crafts, nature hikes, indoor and outdoor games, and storytime. The Adventure Day Camp for children seven to twelve offers team sports, swimming instruction, a mini-Olympics, treasure hunts, waterslide fun, and watermelon polo. Teens enjoy the Explorer program which is designed to challenge while building confidence, initiative, and team work. The challenging ropes course, scavenger hunts, volleyball, moonlight watersliding, hikes, dances, and orienteering are all part of the fun. Young children, newborn to six years, may be cared for in Alice's Wonderland, a licensed child care center in The Village. Children's facilities include a half acre pirate ship playground with an 18 foot high pirate ship, a fort with a maze of ramparts and towers, a wave slide, and a 35 foot tube slide. The Giant Rapid River Ride, a 300-foot waterslide that starts 26 feet in the air, the Turtle Slide, and an Olympic-sized pool are located in one of the resort's two aqua centers.

Ages: 3-17 years old.

Days: Daily from Memorial Day through Labor Day.

Hours: 8:30 a.m. to 4:00 p.m.

Cost: Included in the Family Fest Package.

Area Attractions

The resort is one hour or less from Montreal, Stowe, the Shelburne Museum, and the Long Trail.

THE TYLER PLACE

Address: Highgate Springs, Vermont 05460

Telephone: (802) 868-3301, or (802) 868-4291

Location: Located on Lake Champlain, near the Canadian border, the nearest airports are Burlington (41 miles south) and Montreal (56 miles north). Private planes use the Franklin County Airport. Rental cars are available in both major airports.

Lodging: Twenty-seven cottages located on or near the lake, each with a wood-burning fireplace in the living room and from two to four bedrooms. Also available are 23 suites in the inn and guesthouses.

Rates: $$ Full American Plan (includes breakfast and dinner plus a light luncheon, and most water and land sports).

For Parents

Perched on a grassy Vermont lagoon close to Canada, this 165-acre resort is Nirvana for active families looking for an unpretentious friendly resort atmosphere. There are extensive sports and recreation facilities, plus low-key day and evening entertainment with as much or as little participation as you wish. Included are sailing, windsurfing, tennis, canoeing fishing boats, swimming in a heated pool, and bicycling. Golf is available at three nearby country clubs. Meals are buffet or semi-buffet, with breakfast served practically all morning and leisurely cocktails and dinner served from 6:30 to 8:30. Children typically dine early with their counselors in their own dining room or in alcoves in the main dining room. Families who wish to dine together are also accommodated, and picnic baskets are available any day for you to take out on a canoe paddle, bike trip, or just an outing.

For Kids

The Tyler Place has specialized in family vacations for over 50 years. Their programs are exciting and extensive. Each of their six age-staggered programs is run by college-age counselors and young professionals. The child/counselor ratio varies by age group, from 3:1 for the youngest up to 10:1 for teens. The resort offers morning and evening children's programs with sports instruction, activities, and entertainment geared to the age group. For example, teenagers and older preteens may have water skiing, windsurfing, bumper car rides, soccer, canoe trips, or tennis. Younger children have their own building, lavishly stocked with toys and play equipment. Their activities may include boat rides, water and sand play, arts and crafts, nature walks, and games.

Ages: 2-17 years old, divided into six age groups. Infant care is also available.

Days: Seven days a week from mid-May until mid-October.

Hours: 8:30 a.m. through lunch, and 4:30 p.m. until 8:30 or 9:00 p.m. (10:00 for teenagers).

Cost: Complimentary.

Area Attractions

The resort is one hour or less from Montreal, Stowe, the Shelburne Museum, the Long Trail, and the Champlain Islands. A 5600-acre Natural Wildlife Refuge is across the bay.

South

AMELIA ISLAND PLANTATION

Address: Amelia Island, Florida 32034

Telephone: (800) 874-6878

Location: The Plantation is 29 miles from Jacksonville International Airport. Rental cars are available. Private aircraft may fly directly to Fernandina Beach Municipal Airport four miles north of the Plantation.

Lodging: Accommodations range from one, two, or three bedroom villas, to spacious hotel rooms and suites.

Rates: $$$ Numerous packages are available.

For Parents

Amelia Island Plantation, often referred to as Amelia the Beautiful, consists of clusters of accommodations with a variety of views ranging from a peaceful forest to a manicured fairway or dramatic ocean-front. The clusters are separated by hundreds of yards of lush green lawns, walking paths, and swimming pools. There are dozens of recreational possibilities, but if golf is your pleasure, the Plantation has 45 holes to challenge you. Golf Magazine named Amelia Island Plantation one of the nation's top 12 golf resorts. There are fairways framed by forests, and golf holes on the edge of the Atlantic rimming the beach. If tennis is your game there are 19 Har-Tru, two Deco-Turf, and four Omni courts, including a center tournament court tucked away in a forest of oaks. The tennis center, called Racquet Park, has a pro shop and teaching professionals. There is also a complete fitness center, racquetball courts, and an indoor/outdoor lap pool. Dining at the Plantation can be as casual or as elegant as you are in the mood for. There are many on-site restaurants offering a variety of cuisine, and even a special restaurant just for kids.

114

For Kids

The award-winning youth program at Amelia Island is supervised by counselors who are recreation majors from colleges and universities across the country. All are first-aid trained. The program is grouped by age, three to five, six to eight, and nine to twelve. Three to five year olds take advantage of the beach, fishing in the lagoons, and making handicrafts. Six to eight year olds swim in the pool or ocean, crab, fish, participate in sports, do art projects, and enjoy special theme activities and fieldtrips. Nine to twelve year olds go on field trips, have special instructional workshops in golf, tennis, snorkeling and swimming, enjoy challenging games, complete interesting arts and crafts projects, and engage in many more fun activities.

Ages: 3-12 years old, segregated by age.

Days: Monday through Saturday, seasonally. Spring session is mid-March to the end of April; summer session is Memorial Day through Labor Day. There is also a Thanksgiving program.

Hours: 8:30 a.m. to 4:00 p.m. Three to five year olds have a morning session only. During the summer months, "Just for Kids" restaurant operates from 5:30 p.m. to 9:00 p.m.

Cost: $16.50 per child for full day (includes lunch), $14.00 per child for half day. Five day passes are available at discount rates.

Area Attractions

The Jacksonville Zoo, Jekyll Island Water Park, an evening with the Jacksonville Symphony, or shopping sprees at Jacksonville Landing are all nearby.

THE BREAKERS

Address: One South County Road, Palm Beach, Florida 33480

Telephone: (800) 833-3141, or (407) 655-6611

Location: Palm Beach International Airport is 15 minutes from the Breakers. Rental cars and limousine service are available.

Lodging: Ocean view and garden view rooms and two bedroom suites are available.

Rates: $$$ Both European and Modified American Plans are available.

For Parents

If you go to the Breakers seeking sun and water and sport, you'll find both nature and the facilities to be beautifully accommodating. Architecturally, The Breakers is quite literally a design masterpiece - a structure that was built in 1926, inspired by the Italian Renaissance, and fashioned in the manner of the most notable villas in Italy. Ceilings throughout the public rooms are hand-painted Frescoes completed by 75 Italian artists imported from Europe. There are Flemish tapestries on the walls, and great chandeliers of bronze and crystal fill the lobby and dining rooms. Palm Beach has the distinction of being the area of Florida closest to the Gulf Stream. As a result, average year around temperature is 74 degrees. The resort is located along half a mile of private Palm Beach oceanfront. In addition to the beach, the resort has 19 tennis courts, an ocean golf course, a beach club pool and patio, two croquet lawns, golf on another course at nearby Breakers West, plus workouts and massages at the health club. The relaxing side of the resort provides an informal contrast to evenings in the Florentine Room, or to afternoon tea during the winter season.

For Kids

At the Breakers, children's activities are broken into two age groups: Tot Time (two to four years old) and Gator Group (five to twelve years old). The activities for each group vary daily for a week. The Tots on one day may have a sea shell hunt, play Mr. Potato Head, make paper hats, paint shells, launch balloon rockets, have a story time, or leap through Leapin' Lizards. The Gator Group kids may, the same day, play croquet and horseshoes, learn to tie knots, make bracelets, have an over-and-under relay or three - legged race, go for a picnic, and hop in the pool for a Hula-Hoop Swim. Junior golf and tennis clinics are also offered on alternating days as an optional activity. On weekends during the summer and at peak holiday seasons there is a Children's Dinner Club for the Gator Group from 6:30 p.m. to 9:00 p.m.

Ages: 2-4 years old, and 5-12 years old.

Days: Seven days a week year around.

Hours: Tot Time, 9:00 a.m. to 11:00 a.m. and 1:00 p.m. to 3:00 p. m., and Gator Group 9:00 a.m. to 3:00 p.m.

Cost: $5.00 per session for Tots, and $15.00 per day for Gators (includes lunch).

Area Attractions

Fun day trips for families include the science museum, a trip to Dreher Park Zoo, the Norton Art Gallery, and Lion Country Safari.

Buena Vista Palace

Address: P.O. Box 22206, Lake Buena Vista, Florida 32830-2206.

Telephone: (800) 327-2990, or in Florida (800) 432-2920

Location: Located inside Walt Disney World® Village, the resort is 20 minutes from the Orlando International Airport.

Lodging: The 1,028 deluxe rooms and suites of Buena Vista Palace are family-sized, and all have private balconies or patios.

Rates: $$ Several packages are available.

For Parents

As guests of the Buena Vista Palace you are part of the Walt Disney World® Vacation Kingdom. The Palace is a uniquely designed Disney resort environment nestled along the shores of a blue lagoon and interconnected by winding pathways and waterways. It combines an incredible variety of restaurants, lounges, shops, and entertainment of all types. Recreational facilities are extensive, with three swimming pools, a sauna, three lighted tennis courts, an electronic game room, a Jungle Gym playground, horseshoes and volleyball areas, and jogging trails. You and your family also enjoy playing privileges at the three Walt Disney World championship golf courses and Disney's 18-hole junior course designed just for kids. Buena Vista Palace is surrounded by the enchantment of Magic Kingdom® Park, Typhoon Lagoon, and the Disney-MGM Studios Theme Park. Adjacent Epcot® Center features Future World, with its intriguing look into the past, present, and future, and World Showcase has a permanent multinational exposition spotlighting eleven different countries. In the evening, try Pleasure Island, the exciting entertainment complex at the village.

For Kids

The summer youth program at Buena Vista Palace is designed for children ages three to seventeen years old. Planned activities focus on fun through a child's eye, and provide educational and recreation opportunities for all ages. Qualified college trained professionals supervise each of the resort's three programs. Mighty Mites is for three to six year olds and includes treasure hunts, preschool Olympics, puppet crafts and more. Palace Pals, for seven to twelve year olds, enjoy adventure programs, tennis instruction, water relays, crafty creations, and scavenger hunts, to name but a few. Teen Tracks, just for teens, features pool parties, cook outs, tournaments, and water volleyball.

Ages: 3-17 years old.

Days: Seven days a week from mid June to mid August.

Hours: Hours vary depending on the program, but two to three hours at a time from 9:00 a.m. to 9:00 p.m. is usual.

Cost: $7.00 per child for Mighty Mites, and $10.00 per child for older children.

Area Attractions

The Disney-MGM Studios Theme Park, Typhoon Lagoon with fifty acres of water fun and excitement, and dozens of specialty shops and restaurants are now part of the Walt Disney World Complex. Other nearby attractions are Sea World, Universal Studios, the Kennedy Space Center, and the Atlantic coast beaches.

THE CLOISTER

Address: Sea Island, Georgia 31561

Telephone: (800) SEA-ISLAND

Location: The Cloister is 70 miles from Jacksonville International Airport. Rental cars or Cloister transportation are available from the airport.

Lodging: Double-bed rooms, larger rooms with a sitting area and wet bar, large oceanfront rooms, or guest house suites are available. Private homes in the Sea Island Cottages area may be rented.

Rates: $$ Rates are Full American Plan (all meals and use of the beach club and other amenities are included). Children under 19 stay free.

For Parents

The Cloister is set amid beautiful gardens and lush foliage on Sea Island just off Georgia's coast. Thousands of acres of unspoiled forest and marshes and miles of roadsides free from commercial development add to the refreshing and inspiring environment. An assortment of activities are available. Golf on any of the three 18-hole championship courses or sign up for Golf Digest clinics. Play tennis in round-robin mixers, take aim and try skeet shooting, go horseback riding, fishing, boating, windsurfing, or swimming in the ocean or in the pool. Or perhaps just lounging in the sun by the pool with a good book is your pleasure. The Beach Club and pool are part of a complete spa and fitness center that includes miles of jogging trails. Bicycles for the whole family are offered for rent. Sample true southern cuisine, or ride a jeep train to a plantation supper. Dress up for dinner, or choose informal dress and dining at the Beach Club. After-dinner activities include nightly dancing to The Cloister orchestra and special activities like bingo, concerts, parties, lectures, and games.

For Kids

Children's Playtime at the Cloister is designed for children ages four to eight, and is run by the junior staff. Activities include lawn games, beach play, arts and crafts, swimming, nature walks, and story times. Activities for older children are supervised, but are not scheduled for whole days. For the older ones, there is tennis, sailing, windsurfing, lawn games at specified times, scavenger hunts, boat rides, fishing and crabing parties, beach volleyball, and junior golf clinics. Children over seven and through teenage may prefer the activities for older children. Children 18 and under can play golf and tennis free. During the family festival they also eat free.

Ages: Children's Playtime, 4-8 years old, older children's activities for 9 to teen.

Days: Memorial Day through Labor Day, with selected activities during Spring break and on other major holidays.

Hours: 9:00 a.m. to 3:00 p.m. for Children's Playtime. (Four to twelve year olds may join the children's dinner and playtime from 6:00 p.m. to 9:00 p.m.)

Cost: Complimentary.

Area Attractions

Short trips with family interest would be a day trip to Little St. Simons Island, a boat ride through Sea Island marshes, and an historical tour of Jekyll Island.

Club Med, The Sandpiper

Address: 3500 S.E. Morningside Blvd., Port St. Lucie, Florida 33452

Telephone: (407) 335-4400

Location: Forty-five miles north of Palm Beach International Airport.

Lodging: This resort hotel has six three-story lodges. Each room has a private balcony or terrace, and is designed for double occupancy with two full sized beds and a small refrigerator.

Rates: $$$ Full American Plan. Membership in Club Med is required. Children 4 months to 5 years old stay free certain times of the year.

For Parents

Built along the shores of Florida's St. Lucie river, this 1,000-acre country club style village offers dozens of sports with equipment and instruction. There are 19 tennis courts, nine lighted for night play, and an extensive tennis program offering 2-1/2 hour daily clinics, ball machines, videotaped critiques, and round-robin tournaments. Golf enthusiasts will enjoy the two 18-hole championship courses. A 9-hole pitch & putt course is also right at the village. Just for fun, there is a real circus workshop complete with trapeze and professional instruction. Swim in your choice of five pools, water-ski on the river, work out in the well-equipped fitness center featuring water exercises and aerobics, play volleyball, or go bicycling. Enjoy a refreshing piña colada or other tropical libation at the open-air cocktail lounge, then have dinner in the dining room overlooking the river where both continental and international cuisine are featured. After dinner, a live show and disco provide entertainment into the late evening.

122

For Kids

Mini Clubs are clubs within the main village, expressly built as a paradise for children. Children two through eleven years old are welcomed here to a fully-supervised program of activities from 9:00 a.m. to 9:00 p.m. Kids can come for a whole day or part of the day, or leave for a family activity and then return. Divided by age, there is Petit Club for two and three year olds, Mini Club for four to seven year olds, and Kids Club for eight through eleven year olds. There is also a Baby Club with supervision for infants four to twenty-three months. Activities for kids include a circus workshop, sailing, water-skiing, tennis, golf, arts and crafts, lawn games, scavenger hunts, boat rides, puppet shows, and picnics.

Ages: Mini Clubs, 2-11 years old; Baby Club, 4-23 months.

Days: Daily for Mini Clubs, Sunday through Friday for Baby Club.

Hours: Mini Clubs operate from 9:00 a.m. to 9:00 p.m. Baby Club is available 8:30 a.m. to 6:00 p.m.

Cost: Complimentary.

Area Attractions

The Sandpiper is within driving distance of Palm Beach, Walt Disney World, the Kennedy Space Center, and Sea World. A Walt Disney World resort package is available. For beach outings, regularly scheduled shuttle buses depart every half-hour from the resort.

THE GREENBRIER

Address: White Sulphur Springs, West Virginia 24986

Telephone: (800) 624-6070 or (304) 536-1110

Location: The Greenbrier is eighty miles north and east of Roanoke. Several airlines serve the Greenbrier Valley Airport 15 minutes from The Greenbrier. Rental cars are available at the airport.

Lodging: Hotel rooms, deluxe suites, guest cottages, houses, and estate houses are all available.

Rates: $$ Modified American Plan, includes breakfast and dinner.

For Parents

Nestled in a 6,500 acre estate surrounded by the panoramic beauty of the Allegheny mountains, this resort is a wonderful environment for a totally enjoyable vacation. The vast lobbies of The Greenbrier proclaim a heritage of over 200 years of grandeur and impeccable service. At The Greenbrier you will find a wide range of sports and leisure activities. Golf on any of the three 18-hole championship courses, each with its special challenges as well as breathtaking views of the surrounding mountains. The Greenbrier course was designed by Jack Nicklaus for the 1979 International Ryder Cup Matches, and has also been the site of PGA Senior tournaments. Other available sports include jogging over miles of groomed trails, fishing, trap and skeet shooting, horseback riding, and swimming in the outdoor or indoor pools. If it's tennis you love, play in any season, as there are five indoor and 15 outdoor courts. Each afternoon tea is served in the lobby to the accompaniment of chamber music. Your evening can begin with cocktails and dancing in the Old White Club, the perfect prelude to a wonderful dinner in the Main Dining room or one of the specialty restaurants.

For Kids

Children three to twelve can participate in the Brier Bunch for three to five year olds, or the Sports School for six to twelve year olds. The Brier Bunch may have games and activities, dance and sing, explore The Greenbrier, hear stories, or just play. They are served appropriate snacks mid-morning and mid-afternoon. Children in the Sports School may choose instruction in the sport that is most appealing to them. In addition, creative crafts, outdoor games, bowling, aerobics, hiking, swimming, and putting practice are offered. All activities are supervised by college trained counselors. Children may choose to eat lunch and dinner with their counselors.

Ages: 3-5 years old, and 6-12 year olds.

Days: Daily from Memorial Day through Labor Day.

Hours: All-day program, 9:45 a.m. to 4:00 p.m.; morning session, 9:45 a.m. to 1:00 p.m.; afternoon session, 1:00 p.m. to 4:00 p.m., with an evening program for older children, 6:45 p.m. to 10:00 p.m.

Cost: $20.00 for the all day program, $14.00 for individual sessions.

Area Attractions

Hiking, antiquing, and exploring the beautiful towns of West Virginia are all fun for the whole family.

THE GROVE PARK INN

Address: 290 Macon Avenue, Asheville, North Carolina 28804

Telephone: (800) 438-5800, or (704) 252-2711

Location: The Grove Park Inn is 25 minutes from the Asheville airport. Limousine service, taxis, and car rentals are available.

Lodging: There are 510 rooms in the main inn or in the newer Sammons and Vanderbilt Wings. Most rooms have either garden or mountain views.

Rates: $$$ Several packages are available.

For Parents

Surrounded by the beauty of the majestic Blue Ridge Mountains in Asheville, North Carolina, The Grove Park Inn and Country Club opened its doors in 1913. The gracious inn, a wonderful blend of old-world charm and modern amenities, was built from native boulders. It is now a National Historic Landmark. Since 1984 the inn has been updated with a new heating system, two new wings, and additional facilities to make it a year around resort. Blending with the beauty of the surrounding area is a challenging par 72, 18-hole golf course, a sports center with three indoor tennis courts, squash and racquetball courts, Nautilus equipment, whirlpools and saunas. Six outdoor tennis courts, two swimming pools and an activity center for sports and game equipment are also close at hand. There are full-service pro shops for both golf and tennis, and lessons and clinics are available. The resort also offers carriage rides, and you will find them a special treat for all ages. There are three restaurants on the grounds, one casual and two that require jackets in the evening. After dinner there is entertainment at Elaine's, and a showband offers a wide variety of musical styles from Golden Oldies to Top 40 hits.

126

For Kids

The Grove Park Inn offers two children's programs during the summer months. Teddy Bear Club is for three to five year olds, and Operation Kid-Nap is for six to eleven year olds. Teddy Bear kids fill their day with story-telling, theme days, movies, nature hikes, ice cream making, sing-a-longs, supervised pool play, arts and crafts, and much more. Older kids may have mind-teaser games, lawn and water games, arts and crafts, parachute play, obstacle course races, cookouts, movies, and orienteering. The evening children's program consists of a cookout or pizza party, kickball, flag football, lawn games, frisbee, and four square.

Ages: 3-11 years old.

Days: Monday through Saturday from the end of May to the first week of September for the day programs, Friday and Saturday nights for the evening program.

Hours: 9:00 a.m. to 4:30 p.m., and 6:00 p.m. to 10:30 p.m.

Cost: $17.00 per day per child for the day program (includes lunch), and $15.00 per child for the evening program (includes dinner).

Area Attractions

The nearby Western North Carolina Nature Center is a small zoo and mini-farm with both indoor and outdoor exhibits and a small animal petting area. Another interesting place to visit is the Cherokee Indian Reservation Museum located fifty miles south of Asheville.

HAWK'S CAY RESORT AND MARINA

Address: Mile Marker 61, Duck Key, Florida 33050

Telephone: (800) 327-7775, or in Florida (800) 432-2242

Location: The resort is a 40 minute shuttle flight from Miami, or approximately two hours by car from Miami International Airport.

Lodging: Most guestrooms have views of the Atlantic Ocean or Gulf of Mexico. There are 161 rooms and 16 suites. All rooms have balconies or terraces. Refrigerators are available upon request for a small fee.

Rates: $$$ Rates include an extensive, sixty-item breakfast buffet.

For Parents

Hawk's Cay is located on it's own serene 60-acre island in the five-island Duck Key formation midway down the Florida Keys. Recently refurbished and newly-landscaped, the resort includes a low-slung, rambling West Indies style hotel and 70-slip marina. Hawk's Cay resembles a gracious old estate home. Arriving guests are welcomed informally, and the aim of the resort is to provide casual, unpretentious elegance. There are plenty of entertaining things for you to do, some of them unique to Hawk's Cay, such as swimming with trained dolphins at their training facility, or snorkeling around the only living coral reef in the continental United States. Try deep-sea fishing, or play golf at a nearby club, or maybe just sunning is your favorite pastime. The pool and lagoon are both inviting. The tennis garden has two composition clay courts (lighted for night play) and six hard courts. For dining, Hawk's Cay has four restaurants featuring a variety of cuisines and atmospheres. After dinner, the Ships Pub, located at the marina, operates until the wee hours of the morning.

For Kids

The Kids Club is planned for children age five through twelve during the summer months and some school holidays. Activities may include tiki boat races, scavenger hunts, fishing, dolphin and/or sea lion training sessions, Florida Keys ecology tours, or field trips to other area attractions. Exciting swimming competitions and raft races top off the fun-filled schedule. Daily listings are posted on a poolside chalkboard for the convenience of guests

Ages: 5-12 years old.

Days: Seven days a week from mid June to mid September.

Hours: 10:00 a.m. to 5:00 p.m.

Cost: $10.00 per child per day (includes lunch).

Area Attractions

About 40 minutes to the south is Big Pine Key, home of the Key Deer National Wildlife Refuge inhabited by tiny key deer, alligators, crocodiles, and 526 varieties of birds. At Key Largo, about an hour north, is John Pennekamp Coral Reef State Park. Frequent glassbottom boat tours offer a clear view of an extensive underwater coral garden. Snorkeling and scuba diving are also permissible at the park.

HIGH HAMPTON INN & COUNTRY CLUB

Address: 200 Hampton Road, Cashiers, North Carolina 28717

Telephone: (800) 334-2551, or (704) 743-2411

Location: High Hampton is 63 miles from Asheville and 70 miles from Greenville. Limousine service can be arranged to and from either airport.

Lodging: This resort has 135 rooms and guest cottages, and some privately-owned two and three bedroom vacation homes.

Rates: $$ Full American plan, all meals included.

For Parents

High Hampton is unique in that it is both a charming country inn and a complete resort. The architecture of the inn and guest cottages is rustic, blending well with the natural beauty of the mountains and valley. The resort's main sporting attractions are the golf and tennis programs. During the summer season, you will find that High Hampton offers a series of golf schools varying in length from four to six days. If tennis is your game, a few steps from the inn are eight fast-dry courts and a complete tennis shop. The tennis pro schedules clinics and private lessons. He will also arrange games and round-robin mixers on request. Sailing, canoeing, rowing, fishing and pedal boating are popular water activities, and you will enjoy hiking, and jogging along the miles of professionally-designed fitness trails. From time to time High Hampton conducts creative seminars on quilting, watercolor painting, bridge, fly-fishing, and other interesting subjects. For your dining pleasure, the menu features American cuisine with selected original recipes from their own kitchen. In the evening there is always special entertainment at High Hampton. It may be a movie, a lobby game, or square dancing.

For Kids

The High Hampton children's program is designed to keep youngsters happy and busy. Activities may include games and sports, handicrafts, nature walks, movies, swimming, boating, hiking, and donkey cart rides during the day. Three days a week children's tennis clinics are available. In the evening, the youth director and her assistants take children to dinner or on a hayride or cookout, and then entertain them with games, movies and stories. Although there are no structured programs for teens, there is a teen club which has a stereo, ping-pong and pool tables, and video games.

Ages: 4-11 years old.

Days: Seven days a week from the first of June to the first of September.

Hours: 9:00 a.m. to 2:00 p.m., and 6:00 p.m. to 9:00 p.m.

Cost: $1.00 per child per hour.

Area Attractions

Some great family favorites are horseback riding at Arrowmont Stables (located in the Cashiers area), whitewater rafting with Wildwater Ltd. on the Chattooga River, and railway excursions from Dillsboro to Murphy.

THE HOMESTEAD

Address: Hot Springs, Virginia 24445

Telephone: (800) 336-5771, or in Virginia. (800) 542-5734, or (703) 839-5500

Location: Seventy-five miles from the Roanoke, Virginia airport on US 220.

Lodging: Six hundred rooms including suites, some adjoining, that are suitable for families.

Rates: $$ Modified American Plan includes breakfast and dinner. There is no additional charge for children under three.

For Parents

The Homestead's setting is amid 15,000 acres of the beautiful Alleghany Mountains, a naturally lavish green and blue panorama of mountain and valley, forest, stream, and sky. The Homestead's history is rich. Once Washington and Jefferson strolled here under the trees, as did the Duke and Duchess of Windsor and some of the Rockefeller family. The dining rooms and lounges reflect that elegant style and grandeur that may still be enjoyed today. The facilities are equally impressive on the outside, providing a wealth of outlets for your energies. Three championship golf courses, 19 tennis courts, two outdoor swimming pools, trout fishing in the Homestead's own mountain stream, horseback and carriage riding, skeet and trap shooting, lawn bowling, archery, and just walking through the beautiful Virginia countryside can all be found. Indoors there is a complete up-to-date health spa, eight bowling lanes, and another swimming pool. Also nearby is Warm Springs Pools. In the evening after dining you may take advantage of an evening of dancing, enjoy a current movie, or interact with other guests in a variety of entertaining social activities.

For Kids

Many of the same pleasures adults enjoy as guests of the Homestead are also available to children between the ages of seven and twelve. The youth program, Tower Troop, runs in three-day cycles so that a child can attend several days without repeating. One day may include archery, golf, a visit to the stables, lunch, crafts, water games, and volleyball. The next day may be tennis, a carriage ride, a nature scavenger hunt, nature crafts, swimming, and bowling. In addition to Tower Troop, there is a supervised playground equipped with climbing, riding, and sliding challenges for children three to ten years old.

Ages: 7-12 years old.

Days: Monday through Saturday beginning on Memorial Day and ending on Labor Day.

Hours: 9:00 a.m. to 5:00 p.m.

Cost: $15.00 per day per child.

Area Attractions

The Garth Newell Music Center in Hot Springs sponsors a Summer Chamber Music Festival on weekends. The setting is as beautiful as the music. Many of the musicians have received international acclaim. VEPCO Pumped Storage Project at Mountain Grove is the largest pumped storage dam in the world. Historic Lexington, Virginia is the home of Robert E. Lee and Stonewall Jackson, and the site of the George C. Marshall Museum.

HYATT REGENCY HILTON HEAD

Address: P.O. Box 6167, Hilton Head Island, South Carolina 29938

Telephone: (800) 233-1234, or (803) 785-1234

Location: Hilton Head is located 37 miles from Savannah International Airport. The island has a 3,700-foot lighted runway five miles from the resort.

Lodging: The hotel has 505 deluxe rooms, including 31 one to four bedroom suites. All rooms have refrigerators and balconies.

Rates: $$$ Several packages are available. No charge for children under 18 sharing parent's room, but with a maximum of four persons per room. A second room may be rented for children at a 50% rate reduction subject to availability.

For Parents

The Atlantic Ocean and miles of beach outside your door is your backdrop for beachcombing, soaking up the sun, or playing in the surf. The Hyatt features the island's only Olympic-size pool. In addition, Hyattspa is a splendid health club enclosed under a glass pyramid, complete with an indoor heated pool, whirlpool, sauna, and exercise room. Within walking distance or an easy shuttle ride are the three 18-hole golf courses of Palmetto Dunes Resort and 25 tennis courts at the Rod Laver Tennis Center for both group and individual play. Rent a bike to ride on the easily accessible miles of bike paths meandering through the resort, or rent a canoe for paddling through the scenic network of lagoons that surround the area. Deep sea fishing, wind surfing, and sailing are but a few of the water sports enjoyed on the island. There are a variety of restaurants, and evening entertainment is provided to suit every taste.

For Kids

Called Camp Sand Dollar (a Camp Hyatt), the Hilton Head program includes supervised daily and evening activities for children aged three to fifteen during summers, school holidays, and on weekends. Activities such as sand castle building, crabbing, fishing, bike rides, nature walks, arts and crafts, kite flying, swimming, scavenger hunts, and junior aerobic workouts may be scheduled. A special event on Kids' Night Out may include a trip to play miniature golf, go bowling, or hear Greg Russell's music in Harbourtown. Kids staying at the Hyatt receive a welcome packet that includes a Camp Hyatt cap.

Ages: 3-15 years old.

Days: Daily from May through September, and on weekends during the winter months.

Hours: 9:00 a.m. to 4:00 p.m. and 6:00 p.m. to 10:00 p.m.

Cost: $25.00 for the day session plus a lunch charge. $20.00 for the evening session plus a dinner charge.

Area Attractions

Many land and water tours cover historic Beaufort, Savannah, Charleston, and the Low Country. Hilton Head Island has a multitude of civil war period and ancient Indian relics, as well as four nature preserves and rookeries for viewing the natural wildlife of the area, including 200-pound loggerhead turtles, alligators, bobcats, deer, and wild turkeys.

KIAWAH

Address: P.O. Box 12357, Charleston, South Carolina 29412

Telephone: (800) 654-2924

Location: Twenty-one miles south of historic Charleston on the South Carolina coast. Rental cars are available at Charleston International Airport.

Lodging: Kiawah has 150 rooms at the inn and 300 one to four bedroom villas. Villas have kitchens, washers and dryers.

Rates: $$$

For Parents

Fringed with sand dunes and wild sea oats and bounded by the Atlantic Ocean, Kiawah Island has ten miles of sandy beach to romp on. There are two villages on the island, three golf courses, and 10,000 acres that have been left in their natural state for exploration. The three golf courses offer a scenic and challenging variety of holes. The Turtle Point course was designed by Jack Nicklaus, Marsh Point by Gary Player, and Osprey Point by Tom Fazio. For the tennis enthusiast, there are two separate tennis facilities on Kiawah. West Beach Racquet Club features 14 Har-Tru clay courts plus two lighted hard courts for night play. East Beach Tennis Club has nine Har-Tru courts and three hard courts. There are programs and clinics for all ages. Surrounded by water, it goes without saying that water sports are popular at Kiawah. Overlooking the ocean there are three swimming pools, including one for adults only at the Inn. On the beach you can rent a windsurfer or catamaran, and charter boats for deep sea fishing are available at the marina. Of course there are all the other amenities that you would expect to find, such as bicycling, volleyball, great dining, and lots of evening entertainment.

For Kids

From swimming at the park to exploring the beach, all of the children's activities on Kiawah are supervised by staff counselors in a secure environment. The kid's program takes place at Night Heron Park and is structured for children ages four to twelve. The programs are well organized and educational, with a special emphasis on the environment. One day children may go crabbing and then on a wild animal hunt with their cameras; the next day could include making kites and building sandcastles. Each day there are lots of lawn games and lots of fun.

Ages: 4-12 years old.

Days: During the summer months and major school holidays.

Hours: 9:30 a.m. to 12:30 p.m.

Cost: There is a small fee per child per day.

Area Attractions

Historic Charleston is a city not to be missed. For over 300 years it has been home to pirates, poets, and politicians. Using history to its advantage, Charleston has successfully blended its fascinating architecture with innovative planning and development. Wandering cobblestone streets and along the waterfront promenade you will see fully-restored 18th and 19th century houses, churches, museums, and antique shops. Several homes are open to the public for a small charge. A few blocks inland, browse through an intriguing handmade craft and antique market, or dine in one of the many restaurants in the area.

MARRIOTT'S BAY POINT RESORT

Address: 100 Delwood Beach Road, Panama City Beach, Florida 32411-7207.

Telephone: (800) 874-7105

Location: The resort is a fifteen minute drive from the Panama City Airport. Rental cars are available.

Lodging: There are 200 guest rooms in the hotel, 156 one and two bedroom suites at Loch Legend Village, and 30 one and two bedroom bayfront villas at Lagoon Towers or Harbour Towers.

Rates: $ Several packages are available.

For Parents

Bay Point Resort sits on a tropical wildlife preserve on a peninsula bordered by St. Andrews Bay and Grand Lagoon and overlooking the Gulf of Mexico. The resort's Island Queen, an original Mississippi-style riverboat, carries Bay Point guests to one of Florida's few remaining uninhabited barrier isles—Shell Island. With seven miles of glorious, sun-drenched, sugar-white beach, Shell Island is the ultimate in serenity. But if your preference is to be more active, play golf at either the Lagoon Legend course or Club Meadows, or both! There are complimentary golf clinics to help you cut strokes off your game. Tennis tastes will be satisfied at the tennis center with its 12 Har-Tru lighted courts, and you will find that clinics and matches can be arranged by the pro. For ocean lovers, Bay Point launches deep sea fishing charters, sailing, and snorkeling expeditions daily, or you can rent wave runners. Try fishing from the boardwalk, a bicycle safari, or front lawn croquet. The resort even sports two workout complexes, one within the hotel and the other at the nearby 19th Hole Sports Complex. For dining, Bay Point will tantalize your tastes with seven restaurants and four lounges.

For Kids

The children's program at Bay Point is called the Alligator Point Gang, and is operated by youth recreation specialists. The program is designed for five to twelve year olds. A typical day's schedule may include a nature walk and talk, a shell scouring safari, gator games and snack, wacky water Olympics, and lunch. In the afternoon, kids may have adventures-in-the-air kite flying, beach "wallyball," a leapin' lizards splash party, and treat time. Activities change daily. In the evenings, there are pizza parties, splash parties, and movie mania.

Ages: 5-12 years old.

Days: March through May: Weekends, holidays, and special occasions. June through September: Daily plus an evening program Thursday through Saturday. October through February: Selected weeks.

Hours: 9:30 a.m. to 4:00 p.m. and selected evenings.

Cost: $12.00 per child per day, $20.00 for two children, or $25.00 per family.

Area Attractions

Nearby, family fun is plentiful at Bay Point Sports Park, with outrageous putt-putt courses, batting cages, fishing, and bumper boats. Florida's Caverns State Park is also great.

MARRIOTT'S CASA MARINA RESORT

Address: 1500 Reynolds Street, Key West, Florida 33040.

Telephone: (800) 228-9290, or (305) 296-3535

Location: Five minutes from Key West International Airport. Rental cars are available.

Lodging: There are 314 guest rooms, with 63 suites.

Rates: $$ Several packages are available.

For Parents

The Casa Marina was built at the turn of the century as a beautiful and gracious hotel. With its high vaulted black cypress ceilings, picturesque piazzas and loggias, and Spanish Renaissance arched windows it provides an elegant and nostalgic atmosphere. Today Marriott has restored this legendary hotel to its original beauty and added modern conveniences. Recreation at Casa Marina centers around the sun and the sea. Snorkelers can explore colorful marine life in the clear, calm water off a private beach. There is a fishing pier and a water sports center where Hobie cats, Sunfish, and sailboards may be rented, and where crewed sailing, fishing, and dive excursions are available. You may rent bicycles and mopeds at the resort, too. Other facilities include a good tennis complex, a live entertainment lounge, an exercise club with a sauna, and golf at a nearby course. Nearby Key West offers endless opportunities for dining in outdoor cafes and browsing in boutiques and curio shops. Inhabitants have restored old houses and buildings to their original appearance. There are homes and mansions crafted by skilled ships' carpenters who used square nails, wooden pegs, and chains to withstand high winds. You will notice that many homes have rounded arches, columns with sculptured capitals, and ornately carved gingerbread trims. Strolling around this historic town offers hours of true pleasure.

For Kids

The Casa Marina offers a supervised children's program for about three hours a day, depending on the activities. Creepy critter hunts, face painting, sandcastle building, wiffle ball, arts and crafts, beach play, and treasure hunts are the types of activities offered. In the late afternoon there is usually volleyball on the beach for the older children.

Ages: 5-12 years old.

Days: Daily, year around.

Hours: Generally 11:00 a.m. to 12:30 p.m., and then 1:30 p.m. to 3:00 p.m.

Cost: Complimentary.

Area Attractions:

The Key West Aquarium offers periodic shark feedings and a touch tank where children can reach in and pick up star fish and conchs. The Old Town Trolley and Conch Train are fun ways to see Key West's sites. Boats offer part-day and whole-day snorkeling expeditions to the coral reef off shore. Children will like the East Martello Gallery and Museum, because it brings alive the history of the Florida Keys, and the Old Lighthouse and Military Museum. For the more adventuresome, there is a 70-mile flight by seaplane to the Dry Tortugas, a string of coral islands that are home to 150 species of birds and the Fort Jefferson National Monument, the largest masonry fortress in the western hemisphere. The high point of each day is joining the crowd that gathers at Mallory Pier for the sunset. This is no ordinary sunset watching. Dozens of street performers display skills ranging from puppetry to fire-eating to acrobatics to tightrope walking.

Marriott's Grand Hotel

Address: Scenic Highway 98, Point Clear, Alabama 36564

Telephone: (800) 228-9290, or (205) 928-9201

Location: Forty-five minutes from either the Mobile or Pensacola Airports. Rental cars are available.

Lodging: There are 306 guest rooms with 21 suites and 16 guest cottages.

Rates: $$ Several packages are available.

For Parents

The Grand Hotel is situated among charming turn-of-the-century homes and lush foliage on a large peninsula jutting out from the eastern shore of Mobile Bay on the Gulf of Mexico. Steeped in 143 years of tradition and refined hospitality, the resort offers you an abundance of activities. There are two 18-hole championship golf courses, ten rubico-surfaced tennis courts, a swimming pool, whirlpool and sauna, acres of scenic trails for bicycling, strolling, or jogging, and a 40-slip marina. Horse enthusiasts will enjoy a visit to the Grand's stables and a ride through miles of scenic trails. Water sports include sailing, paddlebikes, and windsurfing. In the afternoon there is usually a game of beach volleyball going on. If you want to try your luck at fishing, the hotel provides a staff member to sit on the wharf and bait hooks! If you catch something, your helper removes the hook, cleans the fish, and takes it to the hotel chef who prepares it according to your specifications and serves it to you for dinner that evening. In the late afternoon, there is an established tradition that you stop in the lobby for afternoon tea before retiring to dress for dinner. You will find that dinners at the Grand are somewhat formal. For gentlemen, a coat is considered suitable attire after 6:00 p.m. Following dinner you can dance the night away to live music in the lounge.

For Kids

Three qualified counselors are available for every ten children in the Grand Fun Camp. During the week the children have a variety of activities which change daily. A sample of a day's activities includes kickball, playground free time, lunch, a piñata party, bingo, and pool fun. Other activities are arts and crafts, fishing contests, puppet making, and lawn games. In the evening, children may get together with their counselors for dinner and a movie if they wish.

Ages: 5-12 years old.

Days: Monday through Saturday from Memorial Day through Labor Day, and major school holidays.

Hours: 10:00 a.m. to 4:00 p.m., and 6:00 p.m. to 10:00 p.m.

Cost: Complimentary except for lunch ($4.00) and dinner ($6.00).

Area Attractions

Bellingrath Gardens, the Gulf Coast beaches, Ft. Morgan, the U.S.S. Alabama, and the Greyhound Dog Track are all fun family outings.

MARRIOTT'S HARBOR BEACH

Address: 3030 Holiday Drive, Fort Lauderdale, Florida 33316

Telephone: (800) 222-6543, or (305) 525-4000

Location: The resort is ten minutes from the Ft. Lauderdale-Hollywood International Airport, and rental cars and limousine service are available.

Lodging: There are 624 guest rooms and suites overlooking the ocean, the pool, or intercoastal waters.

Rates: $$ Several packages are available.

For Parents

Just across the waterway from Ft. Lauderdale lies Marriott's beautiful Harbor Beach resort. Here on Florida's Gold Coast you will never lack things to do. The resort has 1,100 feet of private sandy beach for beach combing, windsurfing, sailing, and sunbathing. Adjacent to the beach is a beautifully landscaped pool and patio area with waterfalls, a poolside bar, a restaurant, and a gift shop. For tennis lovers there are five tropically landscaped outdoor courts and a resident pro who will arrange games, give lessons, or set up a ball machine for you. Golf is available nearby at two 18-hole championship courses. For something a little different, try parasailing, wave runners (similar to jet skis), or water-ski behind a fast boat. The on-site health club has everything you need for your individual fitness program, or you can jog for miles along the beach. The recreation department provides a variety of activities throughout the day, beginning with a morning workout and ending with volleyball on the beach. Dining at the resort varies from casual to formal, and offers a wide variety of cuisine. After dinner there are unlimited entertainment possibilities in the Ft. Lauderdale area.

For Kids

Beachside Buddies is offered for children year around by the recreation staff. Activities may include morning workouts, hula hoop contests, limbo contests, volleyball, coconut bowling, arts and crafts, lawn games, and swimming. There are also a number of beach activities like shell searches, sandcastle building, and playing in the waves. Field trips are offered at least once a week to a nearby attraction such as Ocean World.

Ages: 5-12 years old.

Days: Daily year around, plus Saturday evening programs.

Hours: 10:00 a.m. to 12:00 noon and 1:00 p.m. to 3:00 p.m. On Saturday evenings there are children's activities from 5:00 p.m. to 9:00 p.m.

Cost: $10.00 registration fee (includes a tee shirt).

Area Attractions

Thoroughbred, Greyhound, and Harness racing; Jai Alai, boutiques and shopping at Galleria Mall and Las Olas Blvd. are all fun for the family. Riverboat excursions, sightseeing tours, deep sea fishing, surf fishing, water skiing, windsurfing, and theme parks are also available nearby.

MARRIOTT'S HILTON HEAD RESORT

Address: 130 Shipyard Drive, Hilton Head Island, South Carolina 29928

Telephone: (800) 334-1881, or (803) 842-2400

Location: The resort is located 45 minutes from the Savannah, Georgia, airport. Rental cars are available, as is commercial limousine service.

Lodging: There are 313 guest rooms and 25 suites.

Rates: $$ Several packages are available.

For Parents

Hilton Head Island is really a recreational paradise. With 21 championship golf courses in the area and 200 tennis courts, golf and tennis are year around attractions. Shipyard Plantation, where the Marriott is located, has three 9-hole courses, the Clipper, the Galleon, and the Brigantine. Each course provides a variety of challenges for golfers of all abilities, and clinics and lessons are available. Right next door, the 20-court Shipyard Racquet Club offers everything from private lessons to week-long camps to a complete junior program for all ages. The resort's activities are not limited to courts and courses, however. There are both indoor and outdoor heated pools, a whirlpool spa, and a complete health club with men's and women's locker rooms and saunas. There is also a bike rental stand on the premises, and four miles of beautiful trails for leisurely rides. You can bike or jog along the 12 miles of beautiful uninterrupted beach, too. If being on the water is your passion, nearby marinas rent sailboats and powerboats, or deep sea fishing charters can be arranged. For dining, Pompano's prepares fresh seafood daily, the Veranda serves traditional cuisine and the Patio provides lighter fare. In the Mockingbird Lounge each evening you may listen to live entertainment or dance the night away.

146

For Kids

Kids' World is a supervised program for kids five through twelve that offers a variety of age-appropriate activities. Each day activities are chosen from sandcastle building, beach games, frisbee, volleyball, bike tours, pool games, arts and crafts, relay races, field trips, and sea shell hunts. Teen programs and evening sessions are also available if requested by enough guests. Counselors are all recreation majors with experience in leading young children in outdoor activities. The ratio is one counselor to six children and the children are age grouped if necessary.

Ages: 5-12 years old.

Days: Daily, year around programs.

Hours: 12:00 noon to 4:00 p.m.

Cost: $20.00 per day (includes a picnic lunch).

Area Attractions

A diversity of land and water tours covers historic Beaufort, Savannah, Charleston, and the historic Low Country. The island has a multitude of civil war period and ancient Indian relics. Hilton Head also has four nature preserves and rookeries for viewing the area's natural wildlife, including 200 pound loggerhead turtles, alligators, bobcats, deer, and wild turkeys.

MARRIOTT'S MARCO ISLAND RESORT

Address: 400 S. Collier Boulevard, Marco Island, Florida 33937

Telephone: (800) MARRIOTT, or (800) GET HERE.

Location: The resort is 50 miles south of Southwest Florida Regional Airport in Ft. Myers, and 20 miles from the Naples airport. Luxury coach service is available from either airport. There is also a private runway on the island which operates during daylight hours only.

Lodging: Guest rooms, suites, penthouses, and one and two bedroom villas are available. All accommodations have refrigerators and coffee makers.

Rates: $$ Several packages are available.

For Parents

Nestled amid Florida's ten thousand islands off the southwest Gulf Coast is picturesque Marco Island. The resort is situated on a three-mile crescent of unspoiled white sand beach. A host of activities will keep you entertained whether you prefer swimming in one of the three freshwater swimming pools, enjoying a relaxing soak in a spa, playing tennis on one of the 16 tennis courts, working out in the full service health club, playing volleyball on the beach, or trying your hand at the 9-hole pitch 'n' putt course. For serious golfers, an 18-hole championship course is located nearby. The warm water of the Gulf makes water sports very popular. The resort rents sailboats, Hobie cats, kayaks and water bikes. Windsurfing, water-skiing, and parasailing are also available at the beach. Fishing, both off-shore and on-shore, is excellent on Marco Island where tarpon, kingfish, sea trout, and even snapper can be caught. The resort provides transportation to and from the marina where fishing boats may be chartered for day trips.

148

For Kids

The Marco Island Resort's Beach Buddies program is run by a highly-trained recreation staff. Volleyball, beachball, ping-pong and pitch 'n putt golf are just some of the activities in which kids can participate. Younger children have lots of organized beach activities, as well as scavenger hunts, story time, and arts and crafts.

Ages: 5-13 years old.

Days: During the summer months, and Easter, Thanksgiving, and Christmas school holidays.

Hours: 10:00 a.m. to 4:00 p.m.

Cost: Complimentary.

Area Attractions

There are a number of sights worth seeing on and around Marco Island that are fun for the whole family. There is an hour and a half trolley tour of the island, an all day tour of the Everglades, a trip to a Misccousukee Indian village, airboat rides through the Everglades, and a visit to Thomas Edison's winter home and museum. Nearby Naples is well worth a visit. There artists and artisans have created a series of over 40 shops to display their work.

PGA NATIONAL RESORT

Address: 400 Avenue of the Champions, Palm Beach Gardens, Florida 33418

Telephone: (800) 633-9150

Location: The PGA National is 15 miles north of the West Palm Beach International Airport.

Lodging: There are 335 rooms and 24 one and two bedroom suites, plus 80 cottage suites with two bedrooms and a full kitchen.

Rates: $$$ Several packages are available.

For Parents

The PGA National resort is surrounded by the prestigious PGA National community, with 2,340 acres of manicured fairways, tropical gardens, and a private 26-acre lake. Think of the PGA National and the first thing that comes to mind is golf, and rightly so. There are five tournament quality courses. The most challenging is The Champion, redesigned by Jack Nicklaus, and site of the 1987 PGA Championship. While you may prefer to play the somewhat tamer Haig or Squire courses, The General (designed by and named for Arnold Palmer), is supremely demanding and features one of the most picturesque finishing holes in golf. On the other hand, if your idea of swinging is zinging an ace over a net, the resort has 19 Fast Dry clay courts, twelve with lights for night play, and a fully-equipped pro shop. Also on the grounds is a complete health club with everything you need to keep fit. Swimming in the pools, sailing or kayaking, or fishing for bass are all wonderful water sports. In addition, the complex features five tournament-size croquet lawns for play, plus a full-time pro. There are three restaurants ranging from casual to elegant for dining.

For Kids

Captain Mac's Kid's Camp at the PGA National Resort is designed for ages six to thirteen. Under the supervision of the Activities Director and her crew, they fill their days with arts and crafts, field trips, cookie decoration with the chef, a junior olympiad, a golf lesson, or maybe a limousine ride. Children's golf and tennis clinics are held two days a week, and croquet clinics once a week for an hour each. Captain Mac's Kid's Camp is like an enrichment program. Children may come back with full details on how a hook-and-ladder truck works, or what "men in blue" do, after a trip to the fire station or having a policeman as a guest speaker. A ratio of five children per counselor is maintained, with a maximum group of 30 children.

Ages: 6-13 years old.

Days: Daily for one week at Christmas, two weeks in the spring, and ten weeks during the summer.

Hours: 9:00 a.m. to 5:00 p.m.

Cost: $25.00 per day per child, or $130.00 per week, per child, which covers all admission fees, lunch, snacks, and supplies.

Area Attractions

To the south lies Palm Beach with its glamorous Worth Avenue shops and palatial ocean-front mansions. Slightly north is the Jupiter Dinner Theater. Sports fans can watch Jai-Alai, soccer, polo, baseball, and almost any kind of race from dogs and horses to autos. Cruises along the Intercoastal Waterway are available in the area.

THE RITZ-CARLTON, NAPLES

Address: 280 Vanderbilt Beach Road, Naples, Florida 33963

Telephone: (800) 241-3333, or (813) 598-3300

Location: Six miles north of the city of Naples. Car rental and limousine service is available at the Naples and Regional Southwest Airports.

Lodging: There are 435 guest rooms and 28 suites, including two Presidential suites.

Rates: $$ Golf packages are available during the summer months.

For Parents

Set along the sparkling sands of southwest Florida's Platinum Coast, The Ritz-Carlton offers a natural and undisturbed setting for sports and fitness enthusiasts. The Mediterranean architecture is accented by flower-bedecked courtyards and verandahs overlooking a lush mangrove hammock. There is a formal English rose garden for strolling, and the beach here is three miles of bright white sand, perfect for jogging or stretching out on to catch some sun and relax. For boating enthusiasts, there are sailboats and windsurfers available for rent. As an alternative to the beach, you can enjoy a round of golf at the 27-hole Pelican's Nest golf course, or a game of tennis on one of the six lighted courts. A complete state-of-the-art fitness center is also available for your use. The complex houses a game room with table-top tennis and a 19th-century antique billiard table. Dining at The Ritz-Carlton is flexible, and can range from a six-course celebration dinner to lunch on the beach. Afternoon tea is served in The Lobby, and there is a poolside snack bar for your convenience. After dinner, The Club provides live entertainment for your dancing enjoyment.

For Kids

The Ritz-Kids program at Naples is run by a professionally trained staff and is designed for children ages four to twelve. Daily activities may include sandcastle building and beach play, challenging sports, lawn games, arts and crafts, scavenger hunts, swimming, bike hikes, and a children's dinner theater. All activities depend on the age and interest of the child.

Ages: 4-12 years old.

Days: School holidays, and from Memorial Day to Labor Day.

Hours: 9:00 a.m. to 12:00 noon. Saturday nights there is a Kids Dinner Theater from 6:00 p.m. to 8:00 p.m.

Cost: Most activities are complimentary, however, there is a small charge for field trips and dinner activities.

Area Attractions

There are many nearby exciting places to visit and fun activities to search out for the whole family. A partial list would have to include Collier Automotive Museum, Fleischman Park and Playground, Nautilus Boat Tours, and Wiggins State Park. More information is available at the resort.

SONESTA BEACH HOTEL KEY BISCAYNE

Address: 350 Ocean Drive, Key Biscayne, Florida 33149

Telephone: (800) SONESTA, or (305) 361-2021

Location: The Sonesta Beach Hotel on Key Biscayne is approximately 20 minutes from the Miami International Airport. Rental cars and limousine service are available.

Lodging: The resort has 300 guest rooms and 15 villas. The villas are two, three, and four bedroom houses with a fully-equipped kitchen and private pool.

Rates: $$ Vacation packages are available.

For Parents

The Sonesta Beach hotel on Key Biscayne provides both the ambience of being on a tropical island and the convenience of being just a 15 minute drive to downtown Miami. There are ten Lay-kold tennis courts (three lighted for night play), an Olympic-size pool, and a fitness center on the premises. The fitness center has saunas, steam baths, whirlpools, and aerobics classes. The beautiful white sand beach in front of the hotel is lined with palm trees and chikee huts. Try your hand at sailing; windsurfers and small sailboats can be rented at the beach. Charter expeditions for fishing and diving can be arranged by the hotel. For golfers, the award-winning Key Biscayne Golf Course is just a few minutes drive. Dining at the hotel is at one of four diverse restaurants. The Rib Room serves American cuisine; the Greenhouse is the perfect place for quick, light meals in a patio-like setting; The Snackerie is a beachfront restaurant with picnic-style food; and Two Dragons offers a choice of Japanese or Chinese cuisine. In the evenings there is something for everyone—a quiet lounge, a lively disco for dancing, or a moonlit stroll along the beach.

154

For Kids

The Sonesta Beach Hotel was one of the first hotels to offer supervised children's programs back in 1972. It is called Just Us Kids. The program is for five to thirteen year olds, and runs all day. Children are free to participate in a part day or whole day. Mornings are usually filled with an off-site trip, like roller skating, a trip to the Metro Zoo, Monkey Jungle, or Seaquarium. Lunch is at the Snackerie on the beach. Afternoons are filled with beach and pool activities like penny dives and water basketball. An evening program with dinner, crafts, mini-golf, and movies is also available. During holiday weeks, teens are offered deep sea fishing, windsurfing clinics, tennis, volleyball, and teen Olympics.

Ages: 5-13 years old, with teen programs during holiday weeks.

Days: Daily.

Hours: 10:00 a.m. to 10:00 p.m., with a break at 5:00 p.m.

Cost: Complimentary except for admissions fees and meal costs.

Area Attractions

There are a number of attractions in and around the Miami area for families. Among the more popular are Seaquarium, Planet Ocean, Metro Zoo, Tropical Parrot Jungle, Science Museum, Cradon Canyon Park, and Vizcaya.

SONESTA SANIBEL HARBOUR RESORT

Address: 17260 Harbour Point Drive, Fort Myers, Florida 33908

Telephone: (800) 343-7170, or (813) 466-4000

Location: The resort is on Florida's southwest coast, 25 minutes from the Southwest Regional Airport. Rental cars are available at the airport and at the resort.

Lodging: There are 240 rooms, 49 suites, and 100 luxurious two-bedroom condominiums available.

Rates: $$ Several vacation packages are available.

For Parents

The Sonesta Sanibel Harbour Resort and Spa bills itself as "A Room with a View," and indeed it is. All 240 rooms have a breathtaking view of beautiful San Carlos Bay and the barrier islands beyond. Tennis is a very popular sport at this resort. The center-court stadium has a capacity of 5,500 and has been host to the Davis Cup matches. The center also includes an additional 12 outdoor lighted tennis courts. You can choose to swim in a dramatically-set freeform pool overlooking the beach, in an indoor pool, at the 1,000-foot private beach on San Carlos Bay, or even from an on-site boat dock. Water sports like canoeing, kayaking, windsurfing, and aquabikes are available for rent. Deep sea fishing expeditions, sail boats and charter boats can be arranged by the resort. For golfers, several championship courses are located within a few minutes drive, and Sanibel Harbour also houses a huge spa and fitness center with aerobics classes, exercise equipment, whirlpools, lap pools, racquetball courts, steam baths, beauty treatments, and tanning beds. Several restaurants offer both casual and elegant dining, and the lounge features live entertainment each evening.

For Kids

The Sonesta Sanibel Harbour Resort & Spa keeps young guests busy with Just Us Kids. There is a morning session which runs until 12:30 p.m. Children can choose to have lunch with their counselors. The afternoon session starts at 1:30 p.m. Children may attend one or both sessions. Counselor-supervised activities may include picnics, treasure hunts, nature hikes, swimming pool games, sand-castle building, arts and crafts, limbo contests, bike hikes, weekly birthday parties, face painting, pizza parties, and dinner theaters.

Ages: 5-12 years old.

Days: Daily from December 26 to April 21, and Tuesday through Saturday from April 22 to December 24.

Hours: 10:00 a.m. to 4:00 p.m. for the day program. The dinner theater on Friday and Saturday nights runs from 6:00 p.m. until 8:30 p.m.

Cost: Complimentary. Meals are additional.

Area Attractions

There are a number of side trips that would be enjoyable for families. Among them are the J. N. "Ding" Darling National Wildlife Refuge, the Edison House Museum, Jungle Larry's African Safari, and Waltzing Waters.

SOUTH SEAS PLANTATION

Address: P.O. Box 194, Captiva Island, Florida 33924

Telephone: (800) 237-3102, or in Florida (800) 282-3402

Location: Captiva is connected to the mainland by the Sanibel Causeway, and is 30 miles from Southwest Regional Airport in Ft. Myers, Florida. Rental car, taxi, and limousine service are all available. Ground transportation arrangements should be made prior to departure.

Lodging: Guest accommodations range from waterfront hotel rooms to modern villa condominiums and beach homes.

Rates: $$$ Several vacation packages are available.

For Parents

What makes South Seas Plantation so special is that it is a self-contained island. With 330 scenic sprawling acres there is plenty of room for the 600 accommodations, 18 swimming pools, three restaurants, 22 tennis courts, a 9-hole golf course, and a wide array of land and water sports facilities. In this setting, crowds are easily dispersed and seldom seen. Although the resort has modernized many of its facilities in recent years, it has so preserved its tropical tranquility that it virtually remains the secluded enclave it was when pirates first arrived here 100 years ago. Because of its location, with the warm turquoise waters of the Gulf of Mexico on one side and the expansive Pine Island Sound on the other, South Seas Plantation offers everything from windsurfing, water-skiing, and fishing, to a unique backbay photo safari through the nearby mangroves. If you prefer to dine out, there are many pleasant choices, from candlelight to casual. After dinner, The Ships Lantern Lounge and Chadwick's offer spirits, dancing, and live entertainment nightly.

For Kids

Throughout the year South Seas Plantation offers daily activities for children and teens. Pelican Pals is for three to five year olds, held from 9:30 a.m. to noon. The recreation staff teaches the youngsters arts and crafts, swims and plays games with them, and also provides a snack. Captiva Kids is for six to eight year olds, held from 9:30 a.m. to 2:00 p.m., with similar activities on an age-appropriate level as in Pelican Pals. Castaway Club is for children between the ages of nine and twelve featuring swimming, arts and crafts, canoeing, bike rides, and a variety of games. Tropical Adventure is for teens, and offers water activities, a day of shelling and snorkeling on the resort's diving boat, and a wide array of evening activities.

Ages: 3-19 years old.

Days: Daily.

Hours: Varies by program.

Cost: Small charge depending on the program.

Area Attractions

There are a number of island cruises that are fun for the whole family, including the Captiva Island breakfast cruise, or lunch or dinner cruises to Cabbage Key or Useppa Island. There are also sightseeing cruises to Boca Grande and Cayo Costa — Florida State parks.

SUNDIAL BEACH & TENNIS RESORT

Address: 1246 Middle Gulf Drive, Sanibel, Florida 33957

Telephone: (800) 237-4184, or (813) 472-4151

Location: Sundial Beach is located on Sanibel Island, three miles out in the Gulf of Mexico. Fly into Southwest Regional Airport in Ft. Myers, Florida, which is served by several airlines. Rental cars are available.

Lodging: Spacious one and two bedroom suites, or two bedrooms with a den. All have complete kitchens and many have balconies with a stunning view of the Gulf.

Rates: $$

For Parents

There is something mystical about this tiny island paradise. When you first cross over the three-mile bridge from mainland Florida, Sanibel Island begins to cast its magical spell. It's a remote and relaxing place, yet full of natural splendor and bustling activity. You can enjoy a game of tennis or a clinic on one of the 13 courts, or take a private lesson from one of the staff pros. Swim in one of the five pools, or just lounge around in the sun with a good book. There is also boating, fishing, and windsurfing at the beach, and bicycling, jogging, or just strolling along scenic winding nature trails. Nearby is an 18-hole golf course and several wildlife sanctuaries. There are two restaurants at Sundial for your dining pleasure. Open for breakfast, lunch, or dinner, Window's on the Water offers fresh local seafood along with a spectacular view of the Gulf. Also within the complex, Noopie's Japanese Steakhouse provides fine oriental dining. The Sunset Lounge is the hot spot for live evening entertainment.

160

For Kids

The Sundial offers supervised children's programs year around, although their programs during peak seasons tend to be more extensive. The recreation director is a Florida Certified Leisure Professional, and the instructors have degrees in recreation or related fields. The programs are designed for ages three to six, seven to twelve, and teens. The calendar of events changes monthly, so children staying more than one week in a month would be offered repeat programs with some changes in the activities. The year around camps last at least two hours. In peak season, seven to twelve year olds may stay for four hours. Activities are creative and varied. They may include a Care Bear Cookout for young children or a bike ride and picnic lunch for older children There are junior tennis clinics, teen pool parties and much more.

Ages: 3-12 years old, and teens.

Days: Seven days a week, year around.

Hours: Two and four hour camp sessions beginning in the morning. Hourly scheduled programs at various times during the day from 9:00 a.m. to 9:00 p.m. A schedule of events can be requested prior to your visit.

Cost: Fees begin at $3.50, and the highest fee is $15.00. The $15.00 fee is for the four hour camp, and includes lunch and all activities.

Area Attractions

Sanibel is known worldwide for it's shelling. Learn about the shells in an informative lecture and then shell the beaches!

WALT DISNEY WORLD DOLPHIN

Address: 1500 Epcot Resort Boulevard, Lake Buena Vista, Florida 32830

Telephone: (800) 227-1500, or (407) 934-4000

Location: The hotel is a 20 minute drive from Orlando International Airport, in the Epcot Resort Area. Rental cars are available, as well as transportation to and from the airport.

Lodging: The Walt Disney World Dolphin includes 1,509 guest rooms, 140 of which are suites.

Rates: $$ Limited summer season specials offered.

For Parents

The Walt Disney World Dolphin, which opened June 4, 1990, is the newest member of the Epcot® Resort Area. This hotel is a wonderful combination of luxurious function and whimsical fun. You will see monkey chandeliers, giant palm trees with built in benches, fish mobiles (of catfish, dogfish, and even mousefish!) decorating the hotel. Outside, a gigantic waterfall cascades down the building's surface as if it were a fantastic tropical mountain. The hotel is surrounded by the enchantment of Magic Kingdom® Park, Typhoon Lagoon, Epcot Center, and the Disney-MGM Studios Theme Park. In addition, there are three championship golf courses, eight tennis courts, two swimming pools, and a freeform grotto swimming area near a white sandy beach. A complete health club is also a part of the resort. Getting around within the resort complex is easy. An extensive 50-acre lake and waterway chain connects two parks with hotels. Trams, water taxis, or motor coaches will take you anywhere you wish to go. Within the hotel itself there are seven restaurants and three lounges offering everything from funky 50's style fun to international elegance and grand cuisine.

For Kids

To develop Camp Dolphin, the hotel formed an advisory council of twenty young people to brainstorm a wide range of special activities that relate to and complement the hotel activities. For five to twelve year olds, wacky games and relay races, treasure hunts, bike rodeos, tennis clinics, and arts and crafts are all on the agenda. Younger children age three to five are entertained with nature walks, playdough crafts, face painting, moving to music, storybook hour, and making color collages. In the evenings, the Dolphin Dinner Club features themed dinners and activities like Pirate's Adventure, Beach Bash, and Clownin' Around. Still later is Dolphin Movietime complete with popcorn.

Ages: 3-12 years old.

Days: 7 days a week, year around.

Hours: Daily 1:00 p.m. to 11:00 p.m.

Cost: $35 lifetime membership fee includes daily activities. Evening programs are additional, as are meals.

Area Attractions

At the Walt Disney World Dolphin you are only minutes away from The Magic Kingdom Park and Epcot Center. There are also several new attractions in the area. The Disney-MGM Studios Theme Park, Pleasure Island with country and western, rock n' roll and contemporary dance excitement, Typhoon Lagoon, and dozens of specialty shops and restaurants are now part of the Walt Disney World complex. Other nearby attractions are Sea World, Universal Studios and the Kennedy Space Center.

THE WESTIN RESORT, HILTON HEAD ISLAND

Address: Port Royal Plantation, 2 Grasslawn Ave., Hilton Head Island, South Carolina 29928

Telephone: (800) 228-3000, or (803) 681-4000

Location: Hilton Head Island is 37 miles from Savannah International Airport. The island itself has a 3,700-foot lighted runway for private aircraft. Limousine service and car rentals are available from both airports.

Lodging: Accommodations range from guest rooms and suites to two-and three-bedroom villas.

Rates: $$$ Several packages are available.

For Parents

World famous Hilton Head Island is a beautiful blend of sophisticated pleasures, cultural interests, celebrated sports, and soothing natural beauty. It is an island known for its shops and restaurants, and for its serene tidal marshes and seemingly endless ocean beaches. There are two challenging 18-hole PGA championship golf courses for you to enjoy, and 16 tennis courts (with all three Grand Slam playing surfaces, lights for night play, and a complete pro shop), a croquet lawn, and three heated pools (one of them indoor). You will find that strolling, sunning, and swimming at the beach are all pleasant ways to while away the hours, but if you grow tired of relaxing and seek more vigorous activity there is a complete health club on the grounds, and many miles of jogging and walking possibilities. Beach chairs, bicycles, and sailboats are available for rent at the beach. There are two main dining rooms at The Westin Resort, The Barony for classic cuisine in a relaxed country French manner, and the Carolina Cafe for more casual dining. Seaside tables and refreshing cocktails can be found at the Playful Pelican.

164

For Kids

The Kids' Korner at The Westin Resort keeps kids ages five to twelve delightfully entertained. Tag, relay races, water balloon tosses, kite flying and croquet are all active games. Arts and crafts may include puppets, masks, frames, or friendship pins. At the pool and beach, the kids enjoy a sand dollar search, alligator races, innertube races, shell collecting, and supervised swimming. During the evening program there is volleyball, movies, charades, board games, and beach walks. The teen and kids programs also offer crabbing, miniature golf, a water park, a trip to Harbour Town, and sunset cruises.

Ages: 5-12 years old.

Days: Daily, Memorial Day through Labor Day, and Friday, Saturday, and Sunday the remainder of the year.

Hours: 9:00 a.m. to 4:00 p. m.

Cost: $10.00 for one child and $5.00 for each additional child in the family. Lunch and dinner are not included.

Area Attractions

A diversity of land and water tours covers Beaufort, Savannah, Charleston, and the historic Low Country. The Island has a multitude of civil war period and ancient Indian relics. Hilton Head also has four nature preserves and rookeries for viewing the area's wildlife, including 200 pound loggerhead turtles, alligators, bobcats, deer, and wild turkeys.

WINTERGREEN

Address: Wintergreen, Virginia 22958

Telephone: (800) 325-2200, or (804) 325-2200

Location: The nearest airports are Charlottesville (about 45 miles to the east) and Lynchburg Municipal (about 50 miles to the south). Rental cars are available at both airports. Limousine service can also be arranged.

Lodging: The resort is comprised of privately owned condominiums and single family homes that range from studio to seven bedrooms. All have fully equipped kitchens and cozy fireplaces.

Rates: $$

For Parents

High atop the Blue Ridge Mountains of Virginia, overlooking the beautiful historic Shenandoah Valley, Wintergreen is a resort where you can relax and find peace of mind all year around. A four-season resort, it will provide all the facilities you would expect to find at a fine vacation retreat. There is Devil's Knob, a challenging championship mountain-top golf course and clubhouse with breathtaking views of the surrounding countryside. Twenty-five tennis courts, over 20 miles of hiking trails, swimming pools, and the Wintergreen spa will fulfill your expectations. At Stoney Creek, the valley community of Wintergreen, you will find a wide choice of exciting activities, including spectacular Stoney Creek golf course, 20-acre Lake Monocan and its attendant park, the Rodes Farm Inn and stables, and more swimming pools, tennis courts, and hiking trails. During the winter months, the resort's 3,800-foot elevation provides perfect conditions for downhill skiing. You'll also find superb dining at a variety of restaurants in the area ranging from continental to casual.

For Kids

Wintergreen offers two children's programs and a modest teen program. Little Levels is for two to five year olds. They can play freely in their own well-stocked playroom, as well as join in organized activities like butterfly walks, music, nature crafts, splashing in the kiddie pool, and climbing on the fort in the playground. Kids in Action for six to twelve year olds is an adventure-packed program that features water rodeos, fishing contests, nature scavenger hunts, tennis, golf, swimming, craft workshops, and a special "Kids in the Kitchen" program hosted by a resort chef. In addition, children will be introduced to Wintergreen's nature program where they will enjoy hands-on learning experiences in Wintergreen's natural paradise. The resort's lifeguard staff supplies the creativity in planning activities for visiting teenagers on weekends during the summer months.

Ages: 2-5 years old and 6-12 years old, plus weekend activities for teens.

Days: Daily from mid-June through Labor Day. Weekends in Spring and Fall. Daily mid-December through mid-March.

Hours: 10:00 a.m. to 4:00 p.m. There is also a "Kids Night Out" during the summer months.

Cost: $17.00 for the first child, $14.00 for each additional child; $11.00 per child after the second day.

Area Attractions

Wintergreen is within easy driving distance of many of Virginia's famous historic, cultural, and scenic attractions. The resort offers a guide to area attractions which is well worth writing for and reviewing prior to your visit.

Indexes

Resorts Listed Alphabetically

171

Resort   Page

Resort	Page

Hawaii

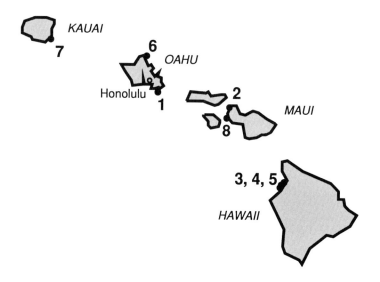

Hawaii

West

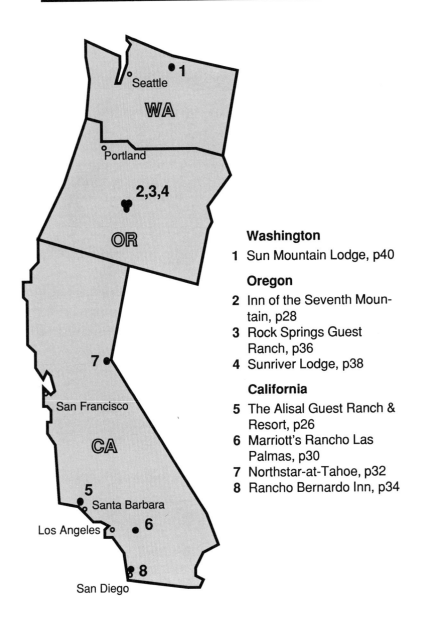

Washington
1 Sun Mountain Lodge, p40

Oregon
2 Inn of the Seventh Mountain, p28
3 Rock Springs Guest Ranch, p36
4 Sunriver Lodge, p38

California
5 The Alisal Guest Ranch & Resort, p26
6 Marriott's Rancho Las Palmas, p30
7 Northstar-at-Tahoe, p32
8 Rancho Bernardo Inn, p34

175

Rocky Mountain

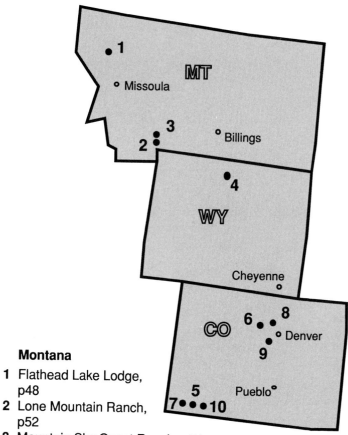

Montana

1 Flathead Lake Lodge, p48
2 Lone Mountain Ranch, p52
3 Mountain Sky Guest Ranch, p54

Wyoming

4 Paradise Guest Ranch, p56

Colorado

5 Colorado Trails Ranch, p44
6 Drowsy Water Ranch, p46
7 Lake Mancos Ranch, p50
8 Peaceful Valley Lodge, p58
9 Tumbling River Ranch, p60
10 Wilderness Trails Ranch, p62

Southwest

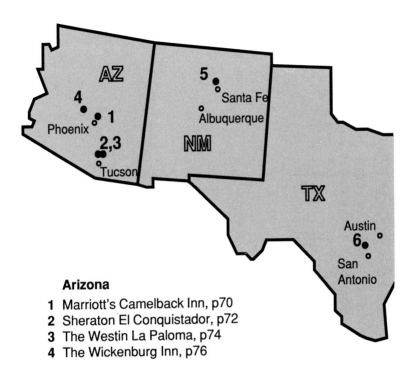

Arizona

1 Marriott's Camelback Inn, p70
2 Sheraton El Conquistador, p72
3 The Westin La Paloma, p74
4 The Wickenburg Inn, p76

New Mexico

5 The Bishop's Lodge, p66

Texas

6 Flying L Guest Ranch, p68

Midwest

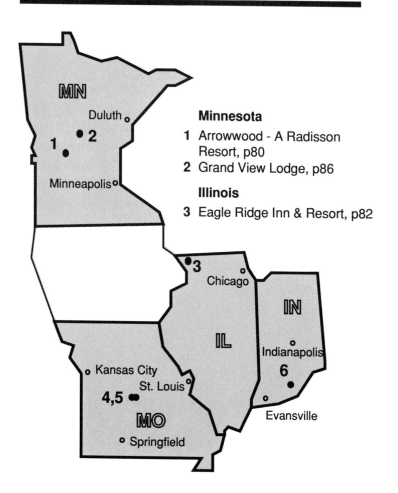

Minnesota
1 Arrowwood - A Radisson Resort, p80
2 Grand View Lodge, p86

Illinois
3 Eagle Ridge Inn & Resort, p82

Missouri
4 The Lodge Of Four Seasons, p88
5 Marriott's Tan-Tar-A Resort, p90

Indiana
6 French Lick Springs Resort, p84

East

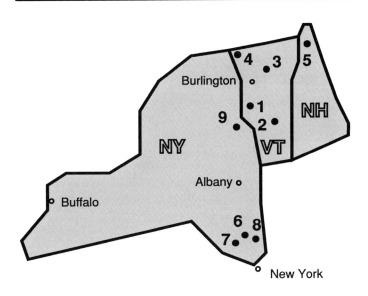

Vermont

1 Basin Harbor Club, p96
2 Hawk Inn and Mountain Resort, p98
3 Smugglers' Notch Resort, p108
4 The Tyler Place, p110

New Hampshire

5 The Balsams, p94

New York

6 Pinegrove Resort Ranch, p100
7 The Pines Resort Hotel, p102
8 Rocking Horse Ranch, p104
9 The Sagamore, p106

South

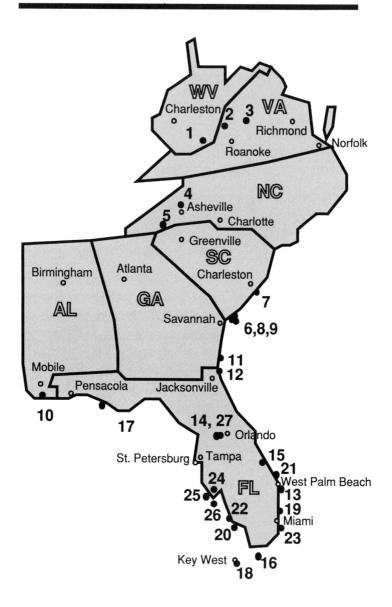

South (cont.)

West Virginia

1 The Greenbrier, p124

Virginia

2 The Homestead, p132
3 Wintergreen, p166

North Carolina

4 The Grove Park Inn, p126
5 High Hampton Inn & Country Club, p130

South Carolina

6 Hyatt Regency Hilton Head, p134
7 Kiawah, p136
8 Marriott's Hilton Head Resort, p146
9 The Westin Resort, Hilton Head Island, p164

Alabama

10 Marriott's Grand Hotel, p142

Georgia

11 The Cloister, p120

Florida

12. Amelia Island, p114
13. The Breakers, p116
14. Buena Vista Palace, p118
15. Club Med,The Sandpiper, p122
16. Hawk's Cay Resort and Marina, p128
17. Marriott's Bay Point Resort, p138
18. Marriott's Casa Marina Resort, p140
19. Marriott's Harbor Beach, p144
20. Marriott's Marco Island Resort, p148
21. PGA National Resort, p150
22. The Ritz-Carlton, Naples, p152
23. Sonesta Beach Hotel, p154
24. Sonesta Sanibel Harbour Resort, p156
25. South Seas Plantation, p158
26. Sundial Beach & Tennis Resort, p160
27. Walt Disney World Dolphin, p162

Readers Recommendation Request

As in all travel experiences, there is no guarantee that your children will be enchanted with the resort programs in this book, but we hope they will be. We included only those resorts we felt had a commitment to quality, and would like to hear from you if you find that they do not. Equally, if the programs are everything that they claim to be and more, we'd like to hear about that too.

If you have a favorite discovery you would be willing to share with other travelers, please let us hear from you and include the following information.

1. Your name, address and telephone number.

2. Name, address and telephone number of "your resort".

3. The resort's brochure (we cannot return material).

Please mail to: Editor's Ink, 2802 E. Madison, Suite 117, Seattle, Washington 98112.

Great
R·E·S·O·R·T·S
FOR PARENTS AND KIDS

Please send me _____ copies of *Great Resorts for Parents and Kids* ® at $12.95 each plus $1.50 for postage and handling. Send to:

Name _____

Address _____

City _____

State, Zip _____

Mail order and payment to:
Editor's Ink
2802 E. Madison, Suite 117
Seattle, Washington 98112.